Play to Grow!

Play to Grow!

Over 200 Games
Designed to Help Your Child
on the Autism Spectrum
Develop Fundamental
Social Skills

Tali Field Berman and Abby Rappaport

2015 Revised Edition

Berman Autism Treatment Center
www.taliberman.com
info@taliberman.com
173 Moshav Aviezer, 99860 Israel

ISBN-13: 978-0-692-52911-9

In memory of Jordan . . .

Whose life was dedicated to creativity
and expressing his own unique self,
which is what we are encouraging
our children to do.

Table of Contents

Acknowledgements. 9

Letter to Parents. 10

Foreword by Jenny McCarthy 11

Part One: Introduction

How to Use This Book. 15

How to Make Games of Your Own 18

Effective Game Facilitation. 21

Part Two: Games in Stages

Stage 1 Games 27

Stage 2 Games 41

Stage 3 Games 53

Stage 4 Games 79

Play Date Games. 105

Stage 5 Games 121

Part Three: Targeted Games

Gross Motor Games 143

Fine Motor Games 149

Appendix A: Additional Strategies for Critical Areas of Growth

6 Steps for Boosting Your Child's Social Skills. 158

Put an End to Challenging Behaviors: Hitting, Biting, Throwing and More 163

6 Strategies to Help Your Child Move Through Anxiety 167

Making the Holidays Work for Your Child 169

Utilizing (Versus Minimizing) Your Child's Differences 171

What Your Child Needs Most to Help Him Grow 173

Bringing the Hidden Miracles to Light. 175

How to Help Your Child Join In 177

Where Does Your Child's Soul Shine? 179

How to Speak to Your Child (and Why It Even Matters) . . . 181

Is Your Child Regressing (and What Can You Do about It) . . 183

Appendix B: Taking Care of You

    Self-Care: 7 Steps to a More Rejuvenated You 186

    Getting Back to the Basics. 189

    Shifting Your Experience to the Now 191

    Move Through Your Fear 193

    Forgive Yourself 195

    How to Navigate Through Daily Life 197

    How to Let Go of Anger 199

    Fear of the Future. 201

Conclusion 203

Index of Games 204

About the Authors 206

Acknowledgements

Thank you to the children, our true inspiration.

Thank you to the parents, our true heroes.

Letter to Parents

Dearest parents and dedicated team members,

It is with great honor and excitement that we present this manual of games to you! In our experience working with children with autism since 1996, we have seen parents and team members investing an incredible amount of energy into creating customized games for their children. The intention of this book is twofold: to assist you by presenting more than 200 fun and purposefully designed games and, of course, to help your children grow to their fullest capacity within the most fundamental areas of social development.

Since the original publication of *Play to Grow!* in 2008, we have learned a tremendous amount as professionals in the autism field. We are thrilled to share this revised edition, which includes more than 30 new games and an appendix of articles offering additional strategies for critical areas of growth and essential steps for taking care of YOU (yes, it is time to make self-care a priority)!

It is our hope that this manual of games will help create many opportunities for deep and meaningful interaction with your child.

Have fun playing!

—Tali Field Berman and Abby Rappaport

Foreword

By Jenny McCarthy

I have played many roles in my life. You might know me as a comedian, actress, host, or best-selling author. Of all these roles, none has been as meaningful and life-changing as being a mother.

When my beautiful boy Evan was diagnosed in 2005, I was not given any hope. I was told that there was nothing that could be done—and honestly, I died in that moment. But I knew, deep down, that Evan had huge potential and soon began to realize the extent of my own determination as a "mother warrior." I vowed I would stop at nothing to help him.

So, we began the journey. I sought out all the information I could, spending hours doing research on the Internet. I began implementing a specialized diet and removed gluten and casein. Within two weeks I saw a dramatic change. I began adding supplements and nutrients, and more incredible growth began to develop. Evan began to regain the language he had lost and to connect with me and his surroundings in a way he never had before.

Today, I am in awe as I witness my son mainstreamed into a typical classroom—thriving socially and academically. I have no doubt that biomedical intervention was key in my child's recovery from Autism. I also know that without having coupled biomedical treatment with traditional therapies that helped teach Evan how to play, communicate, and participate, he would not have the incredible skills of making and being a friend and living an independent life as successfully as he does today.

As a parent, I had to learn how to inspire interaction and how to help Evan attain the communication skills necessary to express his wants, thoughts, and feelings. There were hundreds of milestones that he had skipped, and working with Evan to learn each and every skill that comes naturally for other kids was critical.

I only wish I knew about *Play to Grow!* then!

Parents often ask me what gave me strength on the journey with my son. My answer has always been having an image, clear in my mind, of what he would be like when he recovered. I used to imagine him sitting in the back seat of the car babbling away as he shared about his day. I was determined to see that day, and this vision became my driving force and guiding light. Today, I am eternally grateful that this vision has become a reality, and I am moved to tears as I peek in my rearview mirror, watching and listening to him do just that.

It is my hope for you that you, too, will see such a day with your child. And I believe that, along with biomedical intervention, *Play To Grow!* will be an essential resource to help you get there.

Jenny McCarthy is the author of Louder Than Words: A Mother's Journey in Healing Autism *and* Mother Warriors: A Nation of Parents Healing Autism Against All Odds. *She is also the president of Generation Rescue (www. generartionrescue.org) and an influential activist in the world of healing and preventing autism.*

Part One
Introduction

How to Use This Book

We have designed this book to be as simple and user-friendly as possible. Follow these four simple steps in order to get started.

Step I: Determine Your Child's Developmental Stage

You want to begin by determining your child's developmental stage. In general, the stages are broken down as follows:

Stage 1: Is right for your child if your child makes eye contact about 1 time per minute or less, has a vocabulary of 50 speech-like sounds, and has an interactive attention span below 2 minutes.

Stage 2: Is right for your child if your child makes eye contact about 2–3 times per minute, has a vocabulary of 50–150 words, speaks in 2–3 word sentences, can have a 1-loop conversation, and has an interactive attention span of about 3–4 minutes.

Stage 3: Is right for your child if your child makes eye contact about 4 times per minute, has a vocabulary of 150–500 words, speaks in 4–5 word sentences, can have a 2-loop conversation, and has an interactive attention span of about 5–9 minutes.

Stage 4: Is right for your child if your child makes eye contact about 5 times per minute, has a vocabulary of over 500 words, speaks in 6–8 word sentences, can have a 3- to 5-loop conversation, and has an interactive attention span of about 10–20 minutes.

Stage 5: Is right for your child if your child has typical eye contact, has a vocabulary of over 500 words, speaks in more than 8-word sentences, can have a conversation of 6 loops or more, and has an age appropriate interactive attention span.

You may find that your child falls between two stages, in which case look at games in both stages.

Note: Each stage has a specific interactive attention span; this means how long your child will play in an interactive way, not how long he can play a solitary or repetitious game.

Step II: Select

Select the skill within your child's stage that you will be targeting. In this book, the target skill will be referred to as the "challenge." Select a game that focuses on the challenge that you have chosen. For example, if your child is in stage 3, you may choose to work on "Speaking in 4-5-word sentences."

Step III: Adapt

Once you have found a game that addresses that challenge, you may need to **adapt** it to make it more motivating for your child. For example, you may choose the game below:

 Tell Me What You See

Challenge: Speaking in 4- to 5-word sentences

Motivation: Interesting pictures, anticipation

How to Play: Choose 10 pictures (from magazines or the Internet) that would appeal to your child (funny/unusual pictures or pictures of things that your child loves). Put them on a shelf along with a timer/stop watch. Using a timer or stopwatch, give your child one minute to look at and list the different things he sees in as many 4- to 5-word sentences as possible (for example, "I see a woman laughing," "I see a blue dress"). Count the number of 4- to 5-word sentences he can come up with before the time is up. When one minute is up, present the next picture. Continue until your child has seen all the pictures.

Props: 10 pictures, timer/stopwatch.

Possible adaptation: If your child is particularly motivated by food, choose pictures of food, kitchens or restaurants. This way, your child will be more likely to be interested in and willing to play your game.

Step IV: Take Notes

After you and your child have played the game, **take notes** in the "Notes" section for each game in the margin of each page. This space is meant to be used by you and your team members on a regular basis. Use it to write anything that you find useful, like the date a game was played (so that three different people do not plan the same game during one week) or what did or did not work effectively (so that it can be appropriately adapted if played again in the future). Sample "Notes" entries can be found below:

Notes:
July 5, 2015: He liked the game and was especially motivated by score keeping/winning. —Shelly

July 12, 2015: His attention span went longer than the game; bring in 20 cards next time. —Karen

July 17, 2015: Do not bring in the timer/stop watch next time; he became repetitive with it. —Tom

July 19, 2015: Try it again, he was mostly exclusive and only played the game for 3 minutes. —Carrie

Additional Thoughts . . .

A Customized Playroom

For many children on the autistic spectrum, it can be very challenging to filter out external distractions, thereby limiting their ability to focus on learning and interacting with you. The role of the playroom is to make it as easy and enjoyable as possible for your child (and for you!) to focus on interaction so that both of you are making the most of your time together. For this reason, the games in this book are designed to be played, ideally, in a playroom.

If you have a choice of rooms to use for your playroom, use a room that is in a quieter part of the house. However, you do not need to use a separate room. Many families adapt their child's bedroom to be used as their playroom.

Here are some **key features** to make your playroom as effective as possible:

- **Shelves:** In order to make the playroom less distracting and to create as many opportunities for engagement and communication, I recommend hanging shelves for all the toys/snacks/props, etc. The shelves should be in your reach but out of reach for your child. This way you avoid the distraction of toys scattered across the floor.

- **Doors:** Because this room is designed to be the most effective learning environment for your child, you want to help your child stay in it. Therefore, I recommend using a room with a door and, if necessary, a lock on the door. In my experience, once children see what a sensory haven the playroom is (and how much control they have once they are in it), they will drag you in and close the door themselves!

- **Toys:** Most toys are designed to keep children busy by themselves so that parents can do other things. Because of this, many toys are designed to be self-entertaining. You want to have toys with the very opposite intention: *to be as conducive to interaction as possible.* In the playroom, the toys are simply *tools to help your child interact with you.*

Here are some **examples of effective toys** to have in your playroom:

Big mouthed puppets, several books, musical instruments (drums, xylophones, harmonicas, tambourines, etc.), bubbles, costumes (hats, scarves, wigs, etc.), balls (big and small), simple art supplies (paper, crayons, pencils, scissors, tape, stickers), imaginary play toys (pretend food, doctor's kit, etc.), sensory toys (brushes, feathers, lotion for massage, etc.).

Important note: Do not bring any electronics into the playroom (tablet computers, smart phones, etc.). As you probably know, it is impossible to compete with these kinds of devices and remember, the intention is for your child to play and engage with you!

Above all, this is a room designed for you, your team members and your child to enjoy together. For many families, their playroom becomes a special and inspiring place where their child's most powerful growth occurs.

The Creative Closet Prop List

At the beginning of each chapter of games, you will notice the "Creative Closet Prop List." We suggest that you designate a section of your house, or an actual closet, to store creative props. These props will be used by you and your team members during play time. Each list is designed in such a way that you will be able to do any of the games in that chapter once you have collected the props.

Overall, we have designed games that have simple props and are easy to prepare. However, the games do take some preparation. We encourage you to enlist family members to help you. Consider asking those people who have expressed a desire to help, but are not able to work in the playroom (e.g., a grandmother or sibling). You can also ask your team members to help build your creative closet by collecting /shopping for any props you may need, or preparing the games ahead of time so that they are ready for use.

Not Just the 5 Stages

Besides creating games for eye contact, communication, interactive attention span, and flexibility, we have included games in other important categories as well. After Stage 4 Games, you will find a guide and games for play dates, so that you have clear guidance in facilitating games with your child and a peer at this crucial stage of development. Additionally, since we have found that motor skills often present a challenge for children on the autism spectrum or with other developmental delays, we have included a section on games specifically addressing gross and fine motor skills.

Gender Usage

Since autism has been diagnosed predominantly in boys (in a striking 4:1 ratio), we decided to simplify the language by using the masculine "he" in all game descriptions. However, this book was designed with all children in mind, boys and girls alike.

Who Should Use This Book?

Although the language used in the book is directed towards parents, (i.e. "your child"), this book is absolutely meant to be used by parents and team members alike.

How to Make Games of Your Own

This book is not only a resource of games to play with your child. We hope that this book will also be a springboard for many new ideas and games that you and your team will create for your child — the possibilities are endless!

Follow these four simple steps in order to make a game of your own.

Step I: Identify the Motivations

Either alone or with other team members, make a list of your child's **motivations.** A sample list can be found below.

Danny's Motivations
- letters
- dinosaurs
- songs/musical instruments
- cars
- dancing
- slapstick
- anticipation

Step II: Identify the Challenges

Make a list of the 4–5 most pressing **challenges** that you want to help your child with. A sample list can be found below.

Danny's Challenges
- eye contact
- asking simple "What," "Who" and "Where" questions
- answering simple "What," "Who" and "Where" questions
- pretend play
- asking for help

Step III: Brainstorm

Choose one motivation (e.g., dinosaurs) and one challenge (e.g., asking simple "Where" questions). **Brainstorm** a way to put the two together, and come up with an innovative game for your child. We have found that although you may be able to plan many games on your own, it is always helpful to brainstorm with someone else. Consider working in pairs during a team meeting so that a partner can help you flesh out your game concept even further. The sky is the limit!

A sample game can be found below:

The Dinosaur Search

Challenge: Asking simple "Where" questions

Motivation: Dinosaurs

How to Play: Choose 6–7 pictures of your child's favorite dinosaurs (i.e., the motivation) from magazines or the Internet and cut them out. Hide the dinosaur cutouts on your body before you go into the playroom. For example, tape one dinosaur under the front of your shirt and another under the back. Tape another one under your hat and one in each sock. Tell your child that you have dinosaurs hiding all over you. Encourage him to ask you "Where is the dinosaur?" (i.e., the challenge) in order to find out where they are hiding. Hand the dinosaur to your child as you model the answer by saying "The dinosaur is in my sock!" Then encourage your child to ask you where the next dinosaur is. Continue the game until your child has found and received all of the dinosaurs.

Props: Pictures of dinosaurs, scissors, tape

Step IV: Evaluate

In this final step, **evaluate** your game and take a minute to consider the following question: What's in it for my child? The answer is, hopefully, the "payoff factor."

The "payoff factor" is what gives you leverage in the game. It is the element of the game that makes it worthwhile for your child to do tasks that are challenging for him. If you challenge your child after he has already received his payoff, then he has no real reason to exert himself. Therefore, it is very important that your request comes FIRST and is then FOLLOWED by a clear payoff for your child.

Consider, for example, the Dinosaur Search game above. It has been specifically designed to incorporate the payoff after the challenge has been met. For example, only after your child asks the "Where" question (his challenge), does he receive his payoff (the dinosaur picture). If you challenge your child after he has already received his payoff (for example, if you give him each dinosaur and then ask him, "Where was the dinosaur?"), then he has no real reason to do what is challenging for him and he is less likely to actually ask a "where" question in an engaged, curious and meaningful way.

Effective Game Facilitation

Since 1996, we have been creating and facilitating games for children at varying developmental levels. Over the years, we began to notice that effective game facilitation was dependent upon certain key factors. We have compiled a list of strategies (relating to both attitude and technique) that we have found to be most important.

Four Essential Elements of Attitude

Attitude is everything: We have seen, time and time again, that attitude is a crucial ingredient to your game's effectiveness.

1. Delight

Only introduce and play games that you find fun yourself. If you do not want to play it, your child probably won't either. Either skip a game that does not appeal to you, or adapt it so that it does seem fun. There is nothing more contagious than sincere enthusiasm.

2. Conviction

When you introduce a game, believe that your child will play it with you! Believe it even if he has never played a game like that before or if he has refused that game twice already. Take a few moments before you introduce the game (and again during the game introduction) to actually visualize your child playing it. Just as your own sincere delight is critical, so too is your conviction. Both essential elements will make it more likely that your child will actually play your game.

3. Persistence

Do not be discouraged if your child refuses to play. "No" does not mean "No — forever," it just means "No — for now." You can always try your game a few minutes later, on another day, or even another week. Try investigating why he does not want to play your game, and then adapt the game in order to make it more inviting.

Our colleague Joanna once introduced a board game to a little girl she was working with. Every day for a week, the little girl rejected the game and asked Joanna to leave it outside the room. On the fifth day, Joanna decided to cut up the game and wrap each piece as if it was a present. In doing so, she adapted the game and totally changed her presentation. Now, the little girl was able to unwrap the pieces one at a time and put the game together like a puzzle — and then she played it!

4. Letting Go

Last but not least, it is important to be unattached to the outcome. No matter how much time it took you to prepare the game, your child may decide not to play it. Remember - the goal is not to ensure that your child will play every game that you bring in, but to give your child the opportunity to play new and different games with you. If your child plays just one out of the five games that you brought in, then think of it this way — he has agreed to play one new game that he has never played before!

Keep in mind that the games are *tools* you can use to promote interaction and further develop social skills with your child. If you have tried several times to introduce/adapt your game, but your child still does not want to play it, be willing to shelve it! Recognize that following your child's interest (whether it means joining an exclusive/repetitive activity or playing another game that appeals to him) will much more likely facilitate an interest in interaction. Without an interest in interaction, your child will not be available to play any game with you — so do not forget the importance of following your child's interest.

Finally, do not allow your attachment to the game to blind you to events that are unfolding. Occasionally, we are so focused on following through with our plans that we cannot see that what we are working so hard to achieve-we are already getting!

I remember introducing a game meant to promote conversational skills. The child was not at all interested in my game and instead wanted to tell me something funny that his mother said to him. I, however, was so determined that he would play my game that I found myself trying to cut off the conversation — so that we could play a game about promoting conversation! I was so attached to my game that I did not even realize that we were already having a natural and spontaneous conversation!

Four Essential Aspects of Technique

1. Presentation

Your success in sparking the interest of your child is largely dependent upon how you present your game. For this reason, it is important to experiment with a variety of presentations. Try to notice what seems to work best for your child. For example, try presenting your games as you enter the playroom (since you will likely have his attention then). Take advantage of your entrance by being *dramatic* and *interesting*. For example, come in carrying a very conspicuous closed bag and say "Do you know what I have in my mystery bag?" You can even come dressed as a clown and say "Hello, I am Goofy the clown and I would like to invite you to my special circus. Please take a seat in this special chair . . ."

Or, you may try simply joining your child for a while and only later introduce the game. Alternatively, try playing the game silently by yourself until your child notices and wants to play it with you.

Some children are much more willing to play a game once they have seen how it works. Experiment with modeling the game with another team member or even a stuffed animal in the room. Modeling makes the game much more concrete for your child and he may be more likely to play it once he knows what it actually entails. There is no right way to present a game — the key is to experiment, notice and utilize what works best for your child in each moment.

2. Utilization of Props

We have seen many games cut short because children became distracted by a prop that was used. For this reason, we encourage you to be incredibly mindful of how you set up and utilize your props throughout the game. The props should lend themselves to as much interaction as possible and not become a distraction.

It is important to experiment with using your props and notice what works best for your child. Since it has been our experience that most children become distracted by arranging, touching and organizing objects, we suggest that you tape certain props (like cards/pictures) to the walls out of your child's reach, and not put them on the table. When this is not possible, we encourage you to put props on the shelf between use. We also encourage you to bring out props one at a time and be careful not to have too many props displayed at once. Your child will maintain a higher level of interest in the game by curiously anticipating the next prop.

However, your child may only be motivated to play a game once he has seen, touched and explored the props that you have brought. In this case, offer the props for your child to explore first and then introduce the game. As mentioned in the presentation of the game, there are no rules- the key is to experiment, notice and utilize what works best for your child in each moment.

Tip: As mentioned above, we suggest that you tape cards/pictures to a wall out of your child's reach, so that he will not be distracted by them. Some parents hang up a large carpeted board for this specific purpose. Any cards/pictures can be hung on the board with Velcro.

3. Customizing the Motivation

Not only is it important that you customize the game during preparation, (e.g., create a special Bingo board with animals instead of numbers) but it is also important to customize the game while you are playing it.

From the moment that you introduce your game, pay close attention to whether your child remains highly motivated. Some signs that your child is not motivated include:

- he is not smiling or laughing
- he has a mostly flat facial expression
- he has low eye contact
- he is easily distracted and/or has a restless body

If you have identified a lack or loss of motivation, change the motivation to better suit your child. To adjust the motivation, you can either make the activities more appealing to your child, or infuse the game with a new motivation altogether. Overall, we have found that slapstick (falling down, bumping into things, funny exaggerated faces or body movements) is a huge motivator for many children.

I was playing a game that involved throwing sticks into the air. The activity that the child was designed to do was to correspond to the number of sticks that fell on their colored side. The child was quickly losing interest and motivation. I fell upon a solution entirely by accident. The next time I threw the sticks up, I suddenly sneezed as they fell. The child laughed, I recognized that I had struck a motivation — and used it! From that moment on, I made sure to emit a big and dramatic sneeze every time I threw the sticks. It worked like a charm — and the child participated with enthusiasm.

4. Customizing the Challenge

Keeping the challenge at the right level for your child will help him stay interested and stimulated, and will help him to not give up and walk away. Although there are no rules, you can use the following guidelines to determine if the level of challenge is right for your child. If you have requested something from your child (e.g., "Say 'bubble'") and he does it easily 3 times in a row, then the challenge is too low. Increase the challenge (e.g., "say 'I want bubble'"). Conversely, if your child has not met your challenge after 4 or 5 requests, then the challenge is too high. Decrease the challenge (e.g., "Say 'Bu'").

One Essential Reflection

Each time you leave the playroom after introducing/playing a game with your child, we encourage you to reflect on the above points. Consider the essential elements of both attitude and technique as you review how the session went. This way, you can note which areas worked well and which areas you can improve upon. With continual self-reflection, you can develop your facilitation skills and become as effective as possible for your child.

Part Two
Games in Stages

Creative Closet Prop List

Crafts/art supplies:

- ☐ Several plastic or cardboard tubes
- ☐ Multicolored balloons
- ☐ Colorful streamers
- ☐ Colorful feathers
- ☐ Poster board (4)
- ☐ Sheets of stickers (6)
- ☐ Markers
- ☐ Tape
- ☐ Face paint (hypoallergenic)

Recommended toys/games:

- ☐ Animal masks (either bought or made with paper plates, string and markers)
- ☐ Animal costumes (ears/noses/tails)
- ☐ Funny gloves
- ☐ Big-mouthed puppets
- ☐ Colorful scarves (3)
- ☐ Hula hoop rings (3)
- ☐ Whistle
- ☐ Large ball (size of a basket ball)
- ☐ Jump rope
- ☐ Bottle of bubbles
- ☐ Spin dish
- ☐ Small beanbags (3)
- ☐ Pom-poms

Other:

- ☐ Massage cream (hypoallergenic, unscented)
- ☐ Massage props (soft brush or washcloth)
- ☐ Large cardboard box (big enough for your child to sit in)
- ☐ Medium-sized cardboard boxes (4)
- ☐ Big beanbag or pile of pillows
- ☐ Large, thin blanket

Stage One Games

 ☆1☆ Massage

Props:
☑ Massage cream
☐ Massage props

Notes:

✓ **Challenge:** Eye contact 27/4/18

Motivation: Massages

How to Play: Bring unscented massage cream into the room and offer to massage your child's hands and feet with the cream. You can also bring in different massage props, such as a soft brush or a washcloth. Massage your child's hands/feet/arms/legs using the pressure that your child likes. Then ask him to look at you for the next massage.

Tip: It is important to give your child a massage only if he permits it and to stop if you see any indication that he does not want it. Also, we have seen that most children like deep pressure and often like deep head squeezes. You can do this by putting one hand on your child's forehead and the other hand in the back of his head, and then giving him a deep squeeze.

 ☆2☆ Spin

Props:
☐ Thin towel
(If your child is highly motivated by spins, visit your local toy store. You can buy a big plastic spin dish that your child can sit in while you spin him.)

Notes:

Challenge: Eye contact

Motivation: Spins

How to Play: Bring in a towel and ask your child to lie on it on his back (if you have a rug in the room, roll up the rug first). Hold one end of the towel and spin him around several times. Then ask him to look at you for the next spin.

Variation: You can spin smaller children by holding them upside down or on your back.

Recommended Purchase: To order a spin dish online, go to www.ed-solutionsdirect.com/active/special_active1.htm.

 ☆3☆ Drop!

Props:
☐ Table or chair
☐ Pile of pillows/ big beanbag

Notes:

Challenge: Eye contact

Motivation: Jumping

How to Play: Offer to pick up your child and put him onto a table or chair in the room. Make a pile of pillows or place a big beanbag on the floor to act as a fluffy landing pad. Lift your child high into the air and drop him onto the fluffy pile. Then ask your child to look at you for the next jump.

☆4☆ Jump Rope Snake

Challenge: Eye contact

Motivation: Tickles, visual stimulation

How to Play: Stand in one corner of the room and ask your child to sit in the opposite corner (Give your child a pillow to sit on to help him focus). Bring in a jump rope and wiggle it on the floor like a snake. Wiggle the snake as you move closer to your child, until the snake tickles him all over. Then go back to your corner of the room and ask your child to look at you in order for you to wiggle the snake again.

Variation: For extended eye contact, ask your child to look at you while you move toward him with the snake. Each time he stops, make the snake freeze. When he looks again, make the snake come to life again and wiggle even closer!

Props:
☐ Jump rope

Notes:

☆5☆ Birthday Blower Blow Out

Challenge: Eye contact

Motivation: Anticipation

How to Play: Ask your child to sit in one corner of the room. You can give him a pillow or bean bag to sit on to help him stay in one place. Go across to the other side of the room and then creep back across to him slowly with a birthday blower in your mouth. Blow gently to make the blower unfurl just a little bit. When you get to your child, let out a big, exciting blow so that the blower makes a sound and tickles your child. Do this several times and then go to back to the other side of the room and wait (with a big animated face) for your child to look at you in order for you to do it again. As soon as your child does look at you, begin creeping toward him. Continue the game for as long as you can.

Variation: You can make the game even more exciting by dressing up in costume, like wearing a birthday hat. You can also work on turn taking and ask your child to be the blower.

Props:
☐ A birthday blower and birthday hat

Notes:

⭐6 The Singing Game

Props:
☐ 5–6 pictures representing your child's favorite song

Notes:

Challenge: Eye contact

Motivation: Songs

How to Play: Collect 5–6 pictures that represent your child's favorite songs (for example, a spider for "Itsy bitsy spider"). Tape the pictures around the room within your child's view, but out of his reach. Point to each picture and sing the corresponding song to your child. After you have demonstrated to your child which song each picture represents, ask your child to look at you for the next song.

⭐7 Fun with Animals

Props:
☐ 3–5 pictures of animals
☐ tape

Notes:

Challenge: Eye contact

Motivation: Animals, big body movements

How to Play: Tape a row of 3–5 different pictures of animals on the wall. Point to each animal in turn and act out that animal for your child. For example, point to the picture of a fish, then make a fishy face and pretend to swim around the room. After you have impersonated each animal, ask your child to look at you before you act out the next animal.

⭐8 Fun with Face Paints!

Props:
☐ Face Paint

Notes:

Challenge: Eye contact

Motivation: Face paint, colors, visual stimulation

How to Play: Place some tubes of face paint on the shelf. Take down one face paint and make a dot somewhere on your face (your cheek, forehead or chin) and put it back up on the shelf. Then ask your child to look at you in order for you to put a dot on the same spot on his face. Continue the game until you are both covered with dots.

Variation: If your child is more motivated by letters, numbers or shapes, you can draw those instead. If your child does not want you to draw on his face, you can ask him to look at you in order for you to paint another picture on your own face.

Tip: Use hypoallergenic face paints and baby wipes for easy removal. Put the face paint back up on the shelf in between each use so your child does not get distracted.

 **Blanket Breeze**

Challenge: Speaking in 1-word sentences

Motivation: Visual stimulation

How to Play: Ask your child to lie down on the floor. Wave a small blanket or scarf over his face and body, in order to visually stimulate him and also give him a cool breeze. Then ask your child to say part of the word "blanket" or the whole word to get the next breeze.

Props:
☐ Various colored blankets and scarves

Notes:

⟨10⟩ **Racecar Driver**

Challenge: Speaking in 1-word sentences

Motivation: Rides

How to Play: Take a box that is big enough for your child to sit in and draw wheels on the sides. Pull or push him around the room in the box. Give your child several rides in his "box car" and then ask your child to say part of the word "ride" or the whole word to get the next ride.

Variation: At the end of each ride you can ask your child to pick a new stuffed animal friend to join him for the next ride. If your child is especially motivated by slapstick, make the ride very bumpy. On each sharp turn, spill him out of the car and see if he can get back in.

Tip: For an easier ride, use a box with handles or make a hole and tie a rope to use for pulling

Props:
☐ Large cardboard box
☐ markers

Notes:

 Instant Animals

Challenge: Speaking in 1-word sentences

Motivation: Animals, anticipation, big body movements

How to Play: Make or buy 3–5 animal masks or costumes (ears/noses/tails sets). Put on each mask/costume and pretend to act like that animal (jump around the room and scratch your armpits like a monkey or crawl around and meow like a cat). Then ask your child to say part of the word "animal" or the whole word in order for you to act out the next animal. If your child is especially motivated by a specific animal, have him say that animal's name in order to see your next performance.

Tip: Put the masks/costumes back on the shelf in between use so that the props do not distract your child.

Props:
☐ 3–5 animal masks and/or animal costumes

Notes:

⭐12 Hot Dog Roll

Props:
☐ Large, thin blanket

Notes:

Challenge: Speaking in 1-word sentences

Motivation: Pressure or squeezes, funny imagery

How to Play: Take a large, thin blanket to use as the hot dog bun. Ask your child to become the hot dog by lying down on the edge of the blanket. Roll him up in the blanket and once is he rolled up, pretend to put condiments on him as you massage him (light "karate chops" can be mustard and massage squeezes can be ketchup) and then pretend to eat him. Pull the end of the blanket in order to roll him out. Then ask your child to say part of the word "roll" or the whole word before you roll him up again.

Tips: We find that most kids like the pressure of being rolled in a blanket. You can adjust the tightness of the blanket depending on what your child wants (with their head sticking out of the blanket, of course!) If your child is hesitant to get into the blanket, model the game using a stuffed animal first.

⭐13 The Cushion Squish

Props:
☐ 2 couch cushions

Notes:

Challenge: Speaking in 1-word sentences

Motivation: Being squished (also known as deep pressure)

How to Play: This game is played best with two big, flat cushions from a sofa. Ask your child to lie down on one cushion and tell him you are going to squish him (if he allows and wants it). Put the other cushion on top of him and then lie on top of it, giving him a nice, long deep-pressure squish. (If he likes it, you can do it for 10 seconds at a time.) Then ask your child to say "squish" or "sit" in order for you to do it again.

Variation: You can also take turns, and your child can squish you.

Most of the kids on the autism spectrum love deep pressure; it can be very calming and organizing for a sometimes disoriented sensory system. Try this game—it's sure to be a hit!

⭐14 Noise Tube

Props:
☐ Plastic/cardboard tube

Notes:

Challenge: Speaking in 1-word sentences

Motivation: Tickles, vibrations, silly sounds

How to Play: Take a long tube (a paper towel tube or a PVC pipe from a hardware store) and make funny sounds through it. You can also use it to talk to your child as he holds it to his ear. Then, ask your child to say part of the word "noise" or the whole word to hear the noise again.

Variation: Your child can put one end of the tube on different parts of his body and feel the tickle of the vibration as you blow through it. Then you can ask him to say "tickle" to get the next tickle.

 ## 15 Ambulance Ride

Challenge: Speaking in 1-word sentences

Motivation: Rides

How to Play: Come into the room dressed like an ambulance (a red hat can be your siren and you can make a siren sound). Offer your child a ride on the ambulance by having him get on your back and then giving him a ride around the room. Then ask your child to say part of the word "ride" or the whole word to get the next ride.

Variation: You can also add a "rescue mission" to each ride. Save a stuffed animal from a burning building or a cat from a tree!

Props:
☐ Red hat

Notes:

 ## 16 Balloon Zip

Challenge: Speaking in 1-word sentences

Motivations: Balloons, big movements/visual stimulation, anticipation

How to Play: Put a bag of colored balloons on a shelf. Blow up a balloon but do not tie it. When the balloon is full, let it go and watch it fly across the room. Ask your child to say part of the word "balloon" or the whole word to see the next balloon fly across the room.

Variation: For an additional challenge, ask your child to specify the color balloon that he wants.

Props:
☐ Multicolored balloons

Notes:

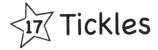 ## 17 Tickles

Challenge: Speaking in 1-word sentences

Motivation: Tickles, anticipation

How to Play: Stand in one corner of the room and ask your child to sit in the opposite corner (give him a pillow to sit on in order to help him focus). Move toward your child slowly from across the room while holding a tickle prop (for example, a puppet, feather, scarf or funny gloves). While you move across the room, say the word "Tickle!" When you get to your child, tickle him! Then ask your child to say part of the word "tickle" or the whole word to get the next tickle.

Props:
☐ Funny gloves
☐ Puppet
☐ Feather/scarf

Notes:

⭐18 Bubbles

Props:
☐ Bubbles

Notes:

Challenge: Speaking in 1-word sentences

Motivation: Bubbles, visual stimulation

How to Play: Use a bottle of bubbles to blow big and small bubbles. Then ask your child to say part of the word "bubble" or the whole word to get the next bubble.

Tip: Keep the container of bubbles on the shelf in between blows so that your child does not try to take the bottle out of your hand.

⭐19 Fall Down

Props:
☐ Objects to trip over (shoe, stuffed animal, toy)

Notes:

Challenge: Speaking in 1-word sentences

Motivation: Slapstick, watching you fall, big body movements

How to Play: Put different props in the middle of the room (you can use a shoe, a stuffed animal or a toy). Walk around the room and pretend to trip over the objects. When you "fall down," make sure to be silly and dramatic. Then ask your child to say part of the word "fall" or the whole word in order for you to do it again.

Variation: Bring dramatic costumes to make your fall even sillier. Your child may love to see a hat, glasses or fake teeth that keep falling off every time you fall!

⭐20 Blow Paint

Props:
☐ 3 cups
☐ Watercolor paints
☐ 3 brushes
☐ 10 pieces of paper
☐ straw

Notes:

Challenge: Speaking in 1-word sentences

Motivation: Visual stimulation (watching the paint spread across the page)

How to Play: Fill three cups with a little water mixed with watercolor paint (make sure each cup has a distinct and vivid color like red, green, and blue). Put a paint brush in each cup and set the cups on the shelf. Tell your child you will make a very neat design for him. Put a piece of white paper on the table and take one of the paint brushes. Drop several pea-sized drops of paint onto the paper. Say "blow," then blow through the straw so that it spreads the paint drop into an interesting design across the paper. Do this several times and then ask your child to say "blow" for you to do it again. Experiment with all the colors on different pieces of paper.

Variation: To help strengthen your child's oral motor skills and muscle tone ,you can ask your child to try blowing through the straw to make the paint design. You can also challenge your child further by asking him to choose which color he would like.

Tip: Make sure to keep the cups of water color paint on the shelf so that it does not become distracting for your child.

 **Blow Ball**

Challenge: Speaking in 1-word sentences

Motivation: Visual stimulation (seeing an object move across the floor)

Props:
- ❏ 5–6 ping-pong balls
- ❏ Straw

Notes:

How to Play: Bring several ping-pong balls and a straw into the room. Stand in one corner of the room and ask your child to sit in the other corner. Say "blow." Then bend down and blow through the straw, pushing the ping-pong ball across the room to your child. Do this several times and then ask your child to say "blow" in order for you to blow through the straw again and make the ball move. Continue until your child has all the balls, and then you can start again!

Variation: To help strengthen your child's oral motor skills and muscle tone, you can ask your child to try blowing through the straw to make the ping-pong ball move toward you.

Interactive Attention Span

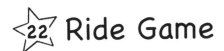 **Ride Game**

Challenge: Interactive attention span of 2 minutes or longer

Motivation: Ride control

Props:
- ❏ Toys
- ❏ Large cardboard box

Notes:

How to Play: In each corner of the room, set up a fun prop that you can use with your child. Make sure that the prop is within your child's view but out of his reach. For example, you might choose a bubble container to blow bubbles, a feather to give feathery tickles, and a balloon to blow up and watch fly away. In the middle of the room, place a cardboard "car" box large enough for your child to sit in. Spin your child in the "car" and ask him to point to the game that he wants to do with you. Once he has chosen the game, drive him to it and play together. Then bring him back to the middle of the room and ask him to point and pick the next game.

 # Freeze!

Props:
- ❏ Colorful streamers/ scarves
- ❏ Whistle

Notes:

Challenge: Interactive attention span of 2 minutes or longer

Motivation: Control, big body movements, visual stimulation

How to Play: Wear a whistle around your neck and tie colorful scarves or streamers to your arms. Dance around the room. After 20–30 seconds, blow your whistle and freeze (holding whatever funny position you are in, even if your hands are over your head and one leg is up!). After each freeze, begin dancing again. Do this several times and then give your child the whistle. Ask him to blow it himself in order to see you freeze for several seconds and then start dancing again.

Variation: Take turns with your child and ask him to dance and freeze whenever you blow the whistle. If the whistle is too difficult for your child to blow, he can bang on a drum instead.

 # Fun with Stickers

Props:
- ❏ Poster board
- ❏ 1 sheet of stickers

Notes:

Challenge: Interactive attention span of 2 minutes or longer

Motivation: Stickers

How to Play: Draw a simple picture of a body on a small poster board. Tape the poster onto the wall out of your child's reach. Put a sheet of stickers onto the shelf. Place one sticker onto the leg of the body drawn on the poster, and put a sticker on your child's leg. Then ask your child to put a sticker on your leg before you put the next sticker on the poster. Continue adding one sticker to the poster and to your bodies until you each have four or five stickers on your bodies.

Activity Toss

Props:
- ❏ Small beanbag
- ❏ Poster board
- ❏ Markers

Notes:

Challenge: Interactive attention span of 2 minutes or longer

Motivation: Throwing, anticipation, silly activities

How to Play: Draw a grid containing six squares on a poster board. In each square, draw a picture of a fun activity you can do together with your child (for example, standing on your head, doing a jumping jack or making funny faces). Then ask your child to throw a beanbag onto a square in order to do the activity drawn there.

Tip: Use tape to make a line on the floor so that your child knows exactly where to stand when throwing the beanbag.

⟨26⟩ Ring Jukebox

Challenge: Interactive attention span of 2 minutes or longer

Motivation: Songs, visual stimulation

How to Play: Slip a hula-hoop ring over your head and wiggle your hips until the ring falls to your feet. As soon as it hits the ground, begin singing your child's favorite song. Do this several times and then ask your child to place the ring over your head in order to hear the next song when it falls to your feet.

Tip: Think of several songs before you begin the game so that you can begin a song as soon as the hula-hoop hits the ground.

Props:
- ☐ Large hula-hoop ring

Notes:

⟨27⟩ Tickle Roll

Challenge: Interactive attention span of 2 minutes or longer

Motivation: Rolling, tickles, anticipation

How to Play: Spread out a towel on the floor in a corner of the room. Ask your child to lie down on it (the towel will help him to focus on remaining in his area). Lie down at the opposite end of the room with a bag full of tickle props. Roll toward your child and ask him to roll toward you. When you meet your child in the middle of the room, give him a tickle with a tickle prop. Roll back to your respective ends of the room and repeat, using a different tickle prop each time.

Tip: Try modeling this game with another person so that your child can see exactly what you will want him to do.

Props:
- ☐ Tickle props (feathers, scarves or puppets)

Notes:

⟨28⟩ The Human Jukebox

Challenge: Interactive attention span of 2 minutes or longer

Motivation: Hearing you sing his favorite song

How to Play: Take five index cards and either write the name of your child's favorite song on each card or draw a picture that would represent your child's favorite song (if your child is not reading yet). Tape the cards on the wall within your child's reach. Prepare a simple cardboard box with a slit cut into it. Ask your child to choose which song he wants you to sing by selecting the card and putting it into the slot. Once he has done that, sing your heart out! Continue until you have sung all the songs.

Variation: If your child is still motivated, you can take turns. You can select and insert each song, and then he can sing it.

Props:
- ☐ 5 cards
- ☐ Marker
- ☐ Cardboard box

Notes:

⭐29 Basketball Cheers

Props:
- ❏ Bucket/box
- ❏ Ball/stuffed animal
- ❏ Tape
- ❏ Pom-poms

Notes:

Challenge: Interactive attention span of 2 minutes or longer

Motivation: Celebrations, basketball, visual stimulation

How to Play: Place a bucket or box in the corner of the room and throw a ball several times into the bucket. Give yourself a big cheer and celebrate each time you throw it in. Then ask your child to throw the ball into the bucket in order to receive his own big cheers. Celebrate all of his attempts to make a basket.

Variation: Use pom-poms for a big cheer after every attempt or basket! Return the pom-poms to the shelf after each cheer so that they do not distract your child. You can also throw stuffed animals into the bucket instead of a ball.

Tip: Use tape to make a line on the floor so that your child knows exactly where to stand when throwing the ball.

⭐30 Beanbag Toss

Props:
- ❏ Beanbag
- ❏ 4 cardboard boxes
- ❏ Markers
- ❏ Tape

Notes:

Challenge: Interactive attention span of 2 minutes or longer

Motivation: Your child's specific motivations

How to Play: Place four open cardboard boxes in the room. Tape a simple picture representing your child's motivations on each box (for example, a picture of bubbles or balloons). Ask your child to try to toss a beanbag into a box. When the beanbag lands in a box (or comes close), let your child do the activity indicated on the box.

Tip: Use tape to make a line on the floor so that your child knows exactly where to stand when throwing the beanbag.

⭐31 Copy Me

Props:
- ❏ Mirrors

Notes:

Challenge: Interactive attention span of 2 minutes or longer

Motivation: Big body movements, slapstick

How to Play: Stand in front of a mirror with your child and move your body in a funny way. For example, wave your arms like a bird or turn around and bend over with your head between your legs. Then ask your child to copy the movement. Once he has, make up a new funny pose for him to copy.

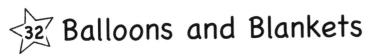

32 Balloons and Blankets

Challenge: Interactive attention span of 2 minutes or longer

Motivation: Balloons, visual stimulation

How to Play: Blow up 3–4 balloons and put them on a thin blanket. Ask your child to hold one end of the blanket while you hold the other end. Raise the blanket upwards together and quickly drop it in order to watch the balloons float down. Then ask your child to help you collect the balloons and put them on the blanket in order to do it again.

Variation: Place different stuffed animals inside the blanket instead of balloons. Watch them fall down each time you wave the blanket!

Props:
- ☐ Several balloons
- ☐ Thin blanket

Notes:

Creative Closet Prop List

Crafts/art supplies:

☐ Colored paper
☐ Markers
☐ Scissors
☐ Tape
☐ Paper
☐ Blank cards
☐ Poster board

Recommended toys/games:

☐ Musical instruments (5)
☐ Puppets
☐ Play tea set
☐ Stuffed animals/dolls
☐ Doctor's kit
☐ Bag of costumes (hats/wigs/glasses)
☐ Play fruits and vegetables
☐ Therapy ball
☐ Bottle of bubbles
☐ Animal picture cards

Other:

☐ Tape recorder
☐ Blank audio tape
☐ Large scarf
☐ Large cardboard boxes (2)
☐ Medium-sized cardboard boxes (4)
☐ Toilet paper
☐ Bottle
☐ Apron

Stage Two Games

33 The Juggling Clown

Props:
- ❏ Colored paper
- ❏ Markers
- ❏ Scissors
- ❏ Tape
- ❏ Ball

Notes:

Challenge: Eye contact

Motivation: Your child's specific motivations

How to Play: Cut out a clown and six ball shapes using colored paper. On the back of each ball, write an activity that would be motivating for your child, like "Spin in circles until you fall on the floor" or "Make a funny face in the mirror". Tape the clown to one wall of the playroom and tape the balls to the other walls. Ask your child to look at you in order for you to take a ball down and read the directions. Do the fun activity together and then tape each ball around the clown on the wall. Continue until the clown has all of his balls! Once he does, you can even pretend to be a clown and do a ball trick, like throwing a ball up in the air and clapping two times before you catch it.

34 Funny Dolls

Props:
- ❏ 5 dolls
- ❏ Shopping bag

Notes:

Challenge: Eye contact

Motivation: Dolls doing funny tricks

How to Play: Set up a small "store" on the shelf with five dolls for sale. Explain to your child that the dolls do not cost money, but they do cost "eye contact dollars". For example, a small doll might cost a 3-second look, while a big doll might cost a 4-second look. Ask your child which doll he would like to buy. Then ask him to look into your eyes for the specified amount of time in order to receive his purchase. When you take the doll off the shelf, have the doll do a funny trick, like jumping up in the air or doing a funny dance. Put the doll into a shopping bag and hand it to your child. Continue until he has "bought" all the dolls.

35 Let's Make Music!

Props:
- ❏ Musical instruments
- ❏ Bag

Notes:

Challenge: Eye contact

Motivation: Music, singing

How to Play: Fill a bag with different musical instruments and put it onto the shelf. Take out the first instrument and play it (you can also sing a song while you play it). Then ask your child to look at you in order for you to play the next instrument in the bag or for you to sing the next verse.

Variation: For extended eye contact, ask your child to look at you for the duration of the entire song. If he looks away, stop playing/singing. You can resume when he looks back at you.

Tip: It is especially useful to model this game for your child with another family/team member first so that your child can see how it works.

⟨36⟩ I Spy with My Eye

Challenge: Eye contact

Motivation: Guessing, anticipation

How to Play: Tape ten interesting pictures on one wall of your playroom (use pictures of objects or characters that your child will likely be motivated by). Ask your child to stand on the other side of the playroom and look at only one picture. Watch his eyes carefully and see if you can guess which picture he is looking at. If you guess it correctly, take that picture down from the wall. Continue the game, but this time you stand across the room and pick a picture to look at. See if your child can guess which picture you chose by tracking your eyes. Continue the game until you have taken down all ten pictures.

Props:
❑ 10 pictures
❑ Tape

Notes:

⟨37⟩ Red Light, Green Light (with a Twist!)

Challenge: Eye contact, looking at your face

Motivation: Anticipation, winning!

How to Play: Stand at one end of the room and ask your child and his friend or sibling to stand at the opposite end. Explain that if you make a certain face (such as closing one eye), that means he is to run toward you. If you make another face (such as opening both eyes), that means to stop. Play the game until one child reaches you first, then take turns.

Variation: To make it especially exciting, you can add an additional motivation for when your child reaches you, like chasing or tickling him.

Props:
None!

Notes:

⟨38⟩ Listening Game

Props:
❑ Tape recorder
❑ Blank audiotape

Notes:

Challenge: Speaking in 2- to 3-word sentences

Motivation: Guessing, funny sounds, anticipation

How to Play: Tape record 5–10 different sounds from outside and around the house (for example, footsteps, dogs barking, cars driving, water running, someone sneezing, etc.). Put the tape recorder onto the shelf. Play the recorded sounds, one at a time, and ask your child to identify the sound. Have your child tell you his guess in a 2- to 3-word sentence (for example, "I hear cars") before you play the next sound.

⟨39⟩ Whose Voice Is That?

Props:
❑ Tape recorder
❑ Blank audiotape

Notes:

Challenge: Speaking in 2- to 3-word sentences

Motivation: Guessing, favorite songs, silly sentences

How to Play: Tape record 5–10 different family or team members saying the same silly sentence or singing your child's favorite song. Put the tape recorder onto the shelf. Play the recordings for your child, one at a time, and ask your child to guess whose voice he hears. Have your child tell you his guess in a 2- to 3-word sentence (for example, "I hear Daddy"). before you play the next voice.

⟨40⟩ Feeling Box

Props:
❑ Medium sized cardboard box
❑ 5–10 different objects to feel

Notes:

Challenge: Speaking in 2- to 3-word sentences

Motivation: Mystery, anticipation

How to Play: Take a medium sized cardboard box and cut out a hole on top (large enough for your child to put his hand through, but not large enough to see what is inside). Put an object in it for your child to feel (for example, a spoon or a cup, etc.). Have your child put his hand through the hole to feel the object. Then ask your child to identify what was inside, and tell you his guess in a 2- to 3-word sentence (for example, "(I) feel a spoon"). Once he has guessed it, put the next object in the box. Continue until your child has identified all the objects.

Variation: If your child is very motivated by numbers or letters, you can put big plastic letters or numbers in the bag/box and have him guess which one he feels.

⭐41 Smelling Game

Challenge: Speaking in 2- to 3-word sentences

Motivation: Smells, anticipation

How to Play: Fill a box or bag with 5–7 different items for your child to smell (such as shampoo or fresh herbs or spices) and put it on the shelf. Designate a special chair for your child to sit in. Ask your child to sit in the "Smelling Chair", close his eyes and bring him one item to smell. Ask him to identify the smell. Have him tell you his guess in a 2- to 3-word sentence (for example, "I smell soap"). Once he has guessed it, bring him the next item. Continue this game until your child has guessed each object by smell.

Tip: If your child is sensitive to smells, choose smells that you know he will like and is familiar with. Avoid using any strong perfumes.

Props:
- ☐ Box/bag
- ☐ 5–7 items to smell

Notes:

⭐42 What's Missing?

Challenge: Speaking in 2- to 3-word sentences

Motivation: Anticipation

How to Play: Tape pictures of 4–5 objects/toys in a row on the wall. Make sure that the pictures are within your child's view but out of his reach. Ask your child to look carefully at all of the pictures and then ask him to close his eyes (or turn around and count to five). While he is not looking, remove one of the pictures from the wall. Ask your child to guess which picture is missing and to tell you his guess in a 2- to 3-word sentence (for example, "(the) ball is missing"). Then show your child if he is correct by revealing the hidden picture. Continue this game by removing a different picture each time

Tip: Start with 3–4 pictures and build up to more as your child progresses.

Props:
- ☐ 4–5 pictures of objects/toys
- ☐ Tape

Notes:

⭐43 Charades

Challenge: Speaking in 2- to 3-word sentences

Motivation: Animals, anticipation, big body movements

How to Play: Choose 7–10 pictures of animals (from a magazine or the Internet) and place them into a bag. Put the bag onto the shelf. Pick a card out of the bag and act like that animal in a funny and exaggerated way. Ask your child to guess which animal you are imitating, using a 2- to 3-word sentence (for example, "You are (a) butterfly"). Then pick the next card and do your next animal imitation. Continue until you have gone through all the cards.

Props:
- ☐ 7–10 pictures of animals
- ☐ Bag

Notes:

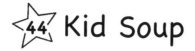 Kid Soup

Props:
- ☐ Large cardboard box
- ☐ Play vegetables/spices
- ☐ Big spoon
- ☐ Apron

Notes:

Challenge: Speaking in 2- to 3-word sentences

Motivation: Being "mixed", imagination

How to Play: Come into the room wearing an apron and place a large cardboard box (to be used as a "soup pot") in the middle of the room and put your child into it. Choose 7–10 items to use as "ingredients" (play vegetables, salt, pepper, etc.) and put them onto a shelf within your child's view. Ask your child which ingredient he would like you to add to the soup pot. Have him tell you his choice using a 2- to 3-word sentence (for example, "I want (an) onion"). Each time you add an ingredient, shake the box (and your child) in order to "mix" the soup. Continue until you have added all the ingredients to the soup pot. Then eat your kid soup!

 Mummy

Props:
- ☐ Toilet paper

Notes:

Challenge: Speaking in 2- to 3-word sentences

Motivation: Control, anticipation

How to Play: Take a roll of toilet paper and ask your child which part of his body he would like you to wrap up like a mummy. Have him tell you what he wants using a 2- to 3-word sentence (for example, "Wrap my legs"). Then wrap that part of his body and repeat the procedure. Continue the game until he is wrapped like a mummy. Then tell him to try to break free!

46 Red Light, Green Light

Props:
- ☐ Nothing!

Notes:

Challenge: Speaking in 2- to 3-word sentences

Motivation: Control, big body movements

How to Play: Ask your child to stand at one end of the room while you stand at the other. Explain to your child that you will only move toward him when he says "green light" and that you will stop when he says "red light." Be sure to let him know that when you reach him, you will tickle him!

Tip: When your child says "green light," run in slow-motion or in a funny way to help the game last longer. Model this game with another family or team member in order to show your child how it works.

⟨47⟩ Secret Box

Challenge: Speaking using verbs and adjectives

Motivation: Your child's specific motivations, anticipation

How to Play: Bring in 5–7 snacks that your child enjoys. Place a big box and a small box onto the shelf within your child's view. Ask your child to close his eyes or turn around. While your child is not looking, put a snack into one of the boxes. Ask your child to guess which box has a snack in it. Have him tell you his guess by saying "Open the big/small box." Open the box that he requested. If he guessed correctly, give him the snack. If he did not, ask him to guess again. Continue the game until you have gone through all the snacks.

Variation: You can also hide the snacks in several different colored boxes and ask him to specify which box he wants you to open, by saying, "Open the red box."

Props:
- ❏ 2 cardboard boxes (one big and one small or two boxes of different colors)
- ❏ 5–7 snacks

Notes:

⟨48⟩ Hot Potato

Challenge: Speaking in 2- to 3-word sentences

Motivation: Sensation of warmth on the body

How to Play: Open your mouth and put it on your child's body like suction. It is important to do this on a part of your child's body that is clothed, like his back while he is wearing a T-shirt. Breathe out slowly, creating a pocket of warm air on your child's body; this is a "hot potato." Give your child several hot potatoes, and then ask him to say "hot potato" in order for you to do it again.

Variation: You can take turns and see if your child can give you a hot potato. You can also work on choice questions by asking 'do you want a hot potato on your leg or on your back?'

Props:
None!

Notes:

⟨49⟩ Bubble Master

Challenge: Speaking using verbs and adjectives

Motivation: Bubbles

How to Play: Put a bottle of bubbles onto the shelf. Blow a large bubble for your child and then blow a few small ones. Ask your child if he would like you to blow another large bubble or lots of small ones. Have him tell you his request by saying, "Blow a big/small bubble." Once your child has answered you, blow the bubble he has requested. Repeat!

Props:
- ❏ Bubbles

Notes:

 Bounce Master

Props:
☐ Therapy ball

Notes:

Challenge: Speaking using verbs and adjectives

Motivation: Bounces

How to Play: Bounce your child on a therapy ball. (If you don't have a therapy ball, you can bounce your child on your knees while sitting in a chair). Give him one large bounce and then a few small ones. Ask your child which kind of bounce he would like next. Have him tell you his request by saying, "Give me a big/small bounce." Once he has answered you, give him the bounce that he requested. Repeat!

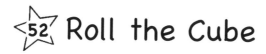 Bye-Bye

Props:
☐ Puppets
☐ Scarf or sheet

Notes:

Challenge: Using greetings (waving goodbye)

Motivation: Puppets, anticipation

How to Play: Hang a scarf or sheet across the room and hide behind it while holding several puppets. Pop up from behind the scarf and have one of the puppets do a funny dance. Then ask your child to wave goodbye to the puppet in order for it to go away. Once your child has waved, have the next puppet pop up to do its dance. Continue until all the puppets have performed.

Tip: Model the waving procedure by waving to the puppet several times and having the puppet wave back.

Interactive Attention Span

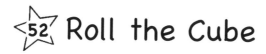 Roll the Cube

Props:
☐ Cardboard box
☐ Markers

Notes:

Challenge: Interactive attention span of 4 minutes or longer

Motivation: Your child's specific motivations

How to Play: Take a square cardboard box and write different motivating activities on each side (for example, "Jump five times," "Sing your favorite song,"etc.). Take turns tossing the box into the air and doing whichever activity the box lands on.

⟨53⟩ Shape Match

Challenge: Interactive attention span of 4 minutes or longer

Motivation: Shapes, colors, completing a picture

How to Play: Draw a picture using a variety of shapes. For example, draw a clown face using circles, triangles and squares. Tape the picture to a wall within your child's view, but out of his reach. Next to the picture, tape paper cutouts of the same shapes you used to create the picture. Ask your child to choose a cutout shape to match the picture on the wall (he can tell you or point to the shape if he does not yet know its name). Pick him up to take the cutout shape that he chose and bring him to the picture to help him tape it where it belongs on the picture. Then, put your child down. Continue until the picture is complete.

Props:
- ❑ Markers
- ❑ Paper
- ❑ Tape

Notes:

⟨54⟩ The Laughing Drum

Challenge: Interactive attention span of 4 minutes or longer (and imitation)

Motivation: Drum and tickles

How to Play: Bring a drum into the playroom and tell your child you will play a simple rhythm on the drum (like hitting it in a slow rhythm three times). Once you have modeled your rhythm, ask your child to do the same rhythm you just did. When he does, give him a wild tickle. Then, play a new rhythm. Continue to play new rhythms and tickle your child after he has modeled the same one you just did.

Variation: This can be done with other instruments your child loves, like a xylophone or tambourine. You can also change the tickle to other motivations like spins or rides.

Tip: You can model how this game works with another team member so your child can see that, when the rhythm is imitated, he'll get a tickle!

Props:
- ❑ Drum

Notes:

⟨55⟩ Tea Party

Challenge: Symbolic play

Motivation: Slapstick, having a tea party

How to Play: Bring a play tea set into the room. Set up a few stuffed animals around a table or a blanket on the floor. Ask your child to pour each animal a pretend cup of tea. As each stuffed animal takes a sip of tea, have it do something funny. For example, the elephant might start jumping around the room, or the teddy bear might fall asleep and snore. Ask your child to pour a cup of tea for each animal in order to watch it do its funny show.

Props:
- ❑ Play tea set
- ❑ Stuffed animals

Notes:

⟨56⟩ Tie Me Up, Cowboy!

Props:
- ❏ 1–2 long ropes
- ❏ Cowboy costumes

Notes:

Challenge: Interactive attention span of 4 minutes or longer

Motivation: Getting tickled by you, watching you struggle to break free

How to Play: Give your child a long rope (like a jump rope) and a cowboy hat. Tell him he is a cowboy and that he needs to tie you up so you cannot break free. If you do break free, you will chase him around the room until you catch him and then tickle him! Begin by asking your child to try to tie your hands or feet (or both!) together as best he can. Then, let him watch as you "struggle" to break free in a very animated way (let this part linger— it's all the fun!). Once you are free, chase your child around until you catch—and tickle!—and him

Variation: Try taking turns and tie him up.

Tip: This game can be best explained by modeling it for your child. Ask a family or team member to play it with you first so he can see how it works.

When my boys were younger, they would often sneak up behind me and tie my feet together while I was washing the dishes. They would squeal with delight watching me try to break free and then chase them around the room. This game was inspired by them.

⟨57⟩ Doctor

Props:
- ❏ Doctor's kit

Notes:

Challenge: Symbolic play

Motivation: Doctor Props

How to Play: Bring in a play doctor's kit filled with a variety of props. For example, you might put in a stethoscope, a jar filled with pretend medicine (the "medicine" can be Cheerios® or a gluten-free substitute if your child is on the GF/CF diet) and bandages. Use costumes to dress up as characters with different medical problems. Act as if you have a cut on your foot, a cough or a case of severe hiccups! Ask your child to treat you by using the different doctor props.

Tip: Model how to use the props first by treating some of the stuffed animals in the room.

58 Huggy Cube

Challenge: Allowing physical affection and interaction

Motivation: Anticipation

How to Play: Take a square cardboard box and tape pictures showing different kinds of physical contact onto each side of the box. For example, you might choose a picture of people hugging, tickling, giving a massage, or patting a child's head. Ask your child to roll the cube and do whichever activity the cube lands on together.

Props:
- ❏ Square cardboard box
- ❏ Pictures
- ❏ Tape

Notes:

59 Spin the Bottle

Challenge: Allowing physical affection and interaction

Motivation: Anticipation, stuffed animals

How to Play: Prepare a deck of 4–5 cards by writing a different physically interactive activity on each one. For example, you might write "Hug your friend" or "Rub your friend's head." Sit in a circle with your child and 5–6 stuffed animals. Pick one of the cards and read it to your child. Put a bottle in the middle of the circle and spin it. Do the activity written on the card with whomever the bottle points to. For example, if the bottle points to the bear, you rub the bear's feet. Then ask your child to pick the next card and spin the bottle.

Props:
- ❏ Bottle
- ❏ 5–6 stuffed animals
- ❏ 4–5 cards
- ❏ Markers

Notes:

Creative Closet Prop List

Crafts/art supplies:

- ☐ Poster board (15)
- ☐ Paper
- ☐ Scissors
- ☐ Tape
- ☐ Markers
- ☐ Blank cards
- ☐ Multi-colored balloons
- ☐ Glitter
- ☐ Envelopes
- ☐ Colored paper
- ☐ String
- ☐ Stickers
- ☐ Craft sticks
- ☐ Bottle caps (14)
- ☐ Velcro®
- ☐ Glue
- ☐ Magnets
- ☐ Rocks (5 medium-sized)
- ☐ Magazines

Recommended toys/games:

- ☐ Play money
- ☐ Wallet
- ☐ Play cash register
- ☐ Doctor's kit
- ☐ Basketball
- ☐ Basketball hoop (or bucket)
- ☐ 5 simple, inexpensive prizes
- ☐ 5–7 piece jigsaw puzzle
- ☐ Stuffed animals
- ☐ Hula hoop
- ☐ Dice
- ☐ Play phone
- ☐ Play tea set
- ☐ Animal picture cards
- ☐ Charades game (for example, Pressman® The Best of Charades for Kids at www.pressmantoy.com)
- ☐ Yoga cards

Stage Three Games

Other:

☐ Face paint (hypoallergenic)
☐ Timer/stopwatch
☐ Pictures of five friends or family/team members (2 each)
☐ Spray bottle
☐ Hair accessories (brush/comb, rubber bands, barrettes, clips, head-bands)
☐ Opaque storage containers (5)
☐ Digital camera
☐ Medium-sized cardboard boxes (4)
☐ Apron
☐ Table cloth
☐ Bag of costumes (hats, glasses, wigs, etc.)
☐ Simple, inexpensive prizes (5–10)

Communication

⟨60⟩ Tell Me What You See

Challenge: Speaking in 4- to 5-word sentences

Motivation: Interesting pictures, anticipation

How to Play: Choose 10 pictures (from magazines or the Internet) that would appeal to your child (funny/unusual pictures or pictures of things that your child loves). Put them on a shelf along with a timer/stop watch. Using a timer or stopwatch, give your child one minute to look at and list the different things he sees in as many 4- to 5-word sentences as possible (for example, "I see a woman laughing," "I see a blue dress"). Count the number of 4- to 5-word sentences he can come up with before the time is up. When one minute is up, present the next picture. Continue until your child has seen all the pictures.

Recommended website: For some interesting pictures, go to www.fotosearch.com, www.funnypictureslady.com or www.acclaimimages.com.

Props:
- ❏ 10 pictures
- ❏ Timer/stopwatch

Notes:

⟨61⟩ Toy Store

Challenge: Speaking in 4- to 5-word sentences

Motivation: Toys, play money

How to Play: Set up a small "store" using a table and a play cash register. Give your child a wallet filled with play money and a shopping bag. Choose some of your child's favorite toys (or buy several new, inexpensive ones) and put them on a shelf. Alternatively, tape 5–10 pictures of your child's favorite characters onto the wall behind you. Make sure that the toys/pictures are within your child's view but out of his reach. Ask your child to tell you in a 4- to 5-word sentence which toy he would like to buy (for example, "I want the blue bear"). Once he has said the sentence, you can proceed with the "sale" and hand him the toy. Continue until your child has bought all the toys.

Props:
- ❏ 5–10 toys
- ❏ Table
- ❏ Tape
- ❏ Shopping bag
- ❏ Play money
- ❏ Wallet and play cash register

Notes:

⭐62 Funny Hair Shop

Props:

☐ Hair accessories

Notes:

Challenge: Speaking in 4- to 5-word sentences

Motivation: Slapstick, control, hairstyles

How to Play: Set up a "hair salon" with a comb/brush and many different types of hair clips, barrettes, rubber bands and headbands. Tape the hair accessories onto the wall or shelf so your child can see them but cannot reach them. Ask your child to tell you what he wants in a 4- to 5-word sentence (for example, "I want the blue clip"). Then use the accessory to style his hair in silly ways. When you are done, look in the mirror or take a picture with a digital camera!

Tip: If your child does not want you to do his hair, he can use a 4- to 5-word sentence to tell you what to do to your own hair (for example, "put on the pink ribbon").

⭐63 Help Mr. Potato Head Get Dressed

Props:

☐ Poster board
☐ Paper
☐ Scissors
☐ Tape
☐ Markers

Notes:

Challenge: Speaking in 4- to 5-word sentences

Motivation: Anticipation, completing a silly picture

How to Play: Draw a picture of Mr. Potato Head and cut out silly paper clothes and accessories (glasses, hats, two pairs of pants, two shirts, two pairs of shoes). Tape the body of Mr. Potato Head onto one side of the wall. Tape the clothes/accessories separately, making sure they are out of your child's reach but easily visible. Encourage your child to choose an accessory/piece of clothing for Mr. Potato Head, and request it using a 4- to 5-word sentence (for example, "I want the red shirt"). Then tape the accessory/piece of clothing onto Mr. Potato Head. Continue until Mr. Potato Head is fully dressed. Then undress him and begin again (or start again using a Mrs. Potato Head)!

⭐64 What's Missing from This Picture?

Challenge: Answering "What?" questions

Motivation: Silly pictures

How to Play: Make/print 10 pictures with missing items. For example, you might choose a bike without a wheel or an elephant without a trunk. Put the pictures onto a shelf and show your child one picture at a time. Ask your child, "What is missing from this silly picture?" Once he has answered, bring down the next picture. Continue until you have gone through all the pictures.

Props:
- ❏ 10 pictures
- ❏ Markers

Notes:

⭐65 Silly Faces

Challenge: Answering "What?" questions

Motivation: Silly faces, characters

How to Play: Make 8–10 pictures of faces with one part missing (for example, a face missing a nose). Cut out all the missing face parts separately and put them into an envelope. Tape one face to the wall and ask your child to look at it carefully. Ask your child "What is missing from this face?" When he answers, give him the missing piece to tape to the face. Continue until all the silly faces are complete!

Props:
- ❏ Paper
- ❏ Markers
- ❏ Envelope
- ❏ Tape
- ❏ Scissors

Notes:

⭐66 What Is Different?

Challenge: Showing interest in other people, identifying changes in detail

Motivation: Funny pictures of family members or friends

How to Play: Before you go into the room, find five people (family or team members) you can photograph. Take a picture of the first person. Then ask that person to make three changes to her/her appearance, like taking off one sock, changing a facial expression, unbuttoning his/her shirt, etc. Take a second picture in which the change can be seen. Do this same with all five people and then print the pictures. Attach the two pictures of each person onto a piece of paper so that you have five pieces of paper. Show these pages to your child one at a time. Ask your child to look closely at both pictures as you ask, "What is different?" See if he can name the three things that are different between the two pictures. Continue through all five pages.

Variation: When you are done, take a picture of your child, ask him to make three changes and then take another picture. Print these pictures, and then your child can ask others if they can find the differences between his two pictures.

Props:
- ❏ Paper
- ❏ Camera
- ❏ 5 people

Notes:

⭐67 Guess What?

Props:
- ☐ Bag/box
- ☐ 10–12 pictures

Notes:

Challenge: Answering "What?" questions

Motivation: Pictures, animals, food, anticipation

How to Play: Choose 10–12 pictures (from magazines or the Internet) of animals, toys, or different kinds of food. Put the pictures into a bag or box and mix them up. Pick a picture, but do not show it to your child. Describe it to your child using three clues, and then ask him "What is it?" When your child guesses it correctly, reveal the picture! Continue until you have gone through all your pictures.

⭐68 A Bag of Goodies

Props:
- ☐ Paper bag
- ☐ 10–12 household items
- ☐ 3 cardboard boxes

Notes:

Challenge: Answering "Where?" questions

Motivation: Anticipation, watching you act, slapstick

How to Play: Fill a large paper bag with 10–12 simple household items taken from different locations in the house. For example, you might choose a spoon/spatula/apron (kitchen), a bottle of shampoo/toothbrush/toilet paper (bathroom) and pajamas/teddy bear/blanket (bedroom). Take three empty cardboard boxes and tape a picture of a house location onto each box. For example, the first box might show a bathroom, the second box, a kitchen, and the third box, a bedroom. Put the paper bag onto the shelf and show your child one item at a time. Ask your child "Where does this belong?" When he guesses the answer correctly, act out a funny scene using that prop. You might pretend to shampoo your hair while singing in the shower or brush your teeth, tongue and lips in a funny, animated way. Then give the prop to your child and ask him to put it into the appropriate box. Continue the game until your paper bag is empty.

⭐69 Where Is the Circle?

Props:
- ☐ 5–8 paper cutouts
- ☐ Poster board
- ☐ Tape

Notes:

Challenge: Answering "Where?" questions

Motivation: Completing a picture, shapes

How to Play: Cut out 5–8 different paper shapes and tape them around the room within your child's view. Prepare a poster by outlining all of the shapes onto it, and tape it to the wall. Have your child sit in a designated chair and ask him to look around the room and locate the shape cutouts. For example, you might ask him "Where is the circle?" When he answers you correctly, give him the shape cutout and let him tape it to the poster within the correct outline. Continue the game until your child has completed the whole poster!

Variation: If your child is more motivated by letters, numbers or pictures of his favorite characters, you can utilize those instead.

⭐70 Puzzle Time

Challenge: Answering "Who/What/Where?" questions

Motivation: Puzzles, characters

How to Play: Take apart a small jigsaw puzzle (5–7 pieces) and put each piece into a separate envelope. Alternatively, cut a favorite picture into five pieces and put each piece into a separate envelope. On the back of each envelope, write a "What?," "Who?," or "Where?" question for your child to answer. You might ask, "What did you eat for breakfast?" "Who plays in your room with you?" or "Where are the books in your room?" Tape the envelopes onto the walls of the room, making sure they are spread out. Ask your child to close his eyes, point out his finger and spin, while you count to 5. At the count of 5, see which envelope your child is pointing to (or is closest to) and ask him the question written on the envelope. After he has answered the question, let him open the envelope and get the puzzle piece inside. When your child has finished answering the questions on all the envelopes, he can put the puzzle together!

Props:
- ☐ 5–6 envelopes
- ☐ Tape
- ☐ Small jigsaw puzzle/ printed picture

Notes:

⭐71 Makeover

Challenge: Answering "What/Where?" questions

Motivation: Face paint, pictures, colors, shapes

How to Play: Come into the room with your face painted. (If your child likes numbers, letters or shapes, you can paint them on your face). Put face paint onto the shelf and show your child the first tube. Ask your child what he would like you to paint on him, or ask him where on his face he would like to be painted. Paint each request. If your child does not like to have paint on his face, then let him decide how to paint your face instead. Wipe your face clean and have him tell you what to paint and where to paint it.

Tip: For extra fun after you have painted your faces, use a digital camera to take pictures of each other.

Props:
- ☐ Face paint
- ☐ Digital camera

Notes:

⟨72⟩ Doctor (Advanced)

Props:
- ❑ Doctor's kit
- ❑ Stuffed animals

Notes:

Challenge: Answering and asking "What/Where?" questions

Motivation: Doctor props

How to Play: Bring in a play doctor's kit filled with a variety of props. For example, you might fill it with a stethoscope, a jar filled with pretend medicine (the "medicine" can be Cheerios® or a gluten-free substitute if your child is on the GF/CF diet) and bandages. Put the kit up onto a shelf and pretend that one of the stuffed animals in the room is hurt. Act out the role of doctor by treating the "sick patient." For example, you might, give a Cheerios® pill to a bear who can't stop sneezing. After your child has watched the "procedure," you can call him over as the next patient. Ask your child "What is hurting you?" or "Where does your body hurt?" When he answers you, respond by treating him with a silly remedy.

Variation: For an additional challenge, let your child act as the doctor. He can ask you the same "What?" and "Where?" questions and come up with the treatment himself.

⟨73⟩ Restaurant

Props:
- ❑ Tablecloth
- ❑ Dishes
- ❑ Apron
- ❑ Paper
- ❑ Pen

Notes:

Challenge: Answering and asking "What?" questions

Motivation: Slapstick, silly food

How to Play: Create a "restaurant" in the room by putting a tablecloth and dishes onto the table. Come in dressed as a waiter wearing an apron. Ask your child to sit at the table and read him the menu of the day (if your child can read, hand him a written menu). Include funny dishes like elephant ear sandwich or frog soup. Ask your child "What would you like to eat?" After he has answered the question, bring him his imaginary meal.

Variation: For an additional challenge, let your child be the waiter and ask you "What do you want to eat?" and bring you a meal! After each round, you can create a new silly menu together and play again.

⟨74⟩ Balloons Galore!

Challenge: Answering "Who/What/Where?" questions

Motivation: Balloons

How to Play: Choose 7–10 different colored balloons, but do not blow them up. Tape them to the wall out of your child's reach. Take 7–10 slips of colored paper to match each colored balloon. On the back of each colored piece of paper, write a "Who/What/Where?" question to ask your child. You might ask "Who is in your family?," "Where do you like to play?," or "What is your favorite food?" After your child answers one of the questions, help him get the matching colored balloon off the wall. Then, blow up the balloon as big as possible, but do not knot it. Let the balloon go so that your child can watch it fly across the room! When the deflated balloon has landed, place it on the shelf and read the question on the next piece of colored paper. Continue the game until you have flown all the balloons.

Props:
- ❒ 7–10 multi-colored balloons
- ❒ 7–10 slips of colored paper

Notes:

⟨75⟩ Feed the Hungry Monster

Challenge: Asking and answering "What?" questions

Motivation: Watching you eat in a silly and animated way

How to Play: Bring in two plates with a different type of cut-up food on each plate (for example, cut apples on one and cut cucumbers on the other). Tell your child you are a very hungry monster but that your hands are very tired and so you need him to feed you. Tell your child to ask you, "What do you want to eat?" Once you answer, have him use a fork to feed you the food you selected. Chew and rub your belly in a very enthusiastic and animated way (you can even make a dramatic burp when you are done—whatever will make it fun for your child). Then ask him to repeat the question before he feeds you the next bite. Continue until you have finished the food on both plates.

Tip: You can help your child understand how the game works by first demonstrating it with another family or team member.

Variation: You can add more plates of different kinds of food to make it more interesting, and as always, you can take turns and work on the skill of asking and answering "What?" questions.

Props:
- ❒ 2 plates
- ❒ 2 types of cut-up food, 1 on each plate
- ❒ fork

Notes:

⭐76 Going to the Cleaners

Props:
- ❏ 5 articles of clothing
- ❏ 5–10 stickers
- ❏ Cardboard box
- ❏ Markers
- ❏ Spray bottle
- ❏ Water
- ❏ Bag

Notes:

Challenge: Asking and answering "What?" questions

Motivation: Silly stains, spraying a spray bottle, shaking an object

How to Play: Draw dials on a large cardboard box in order to make a "washing machine" and set up the box in the room. Take five articles of clothing and create a pretend stain on each piece of clothing by putting a different colored sticker on each one. Put the clothing into a bag and give it to your child. Ask your child to hand you each piece of clothing one by one, as if he was at the cleaners. After your child has given you each article of clothing, ask him what kind of stain is on the clothing (for example, he might say that the stain is from strawberry ice cream). After your child has answered your question, he can help you spray the clothing with a "stain remover" (you can use a spray bottle filled with water). Then put the clothing into the "washing machine" and ask him to help you shake the box in order to "wash" the clothing. Keep shaking until the "stain" comes off (to remove the "stain," take the sticker off). In order for your child to help spray and wash the next one, have him tell you which stain is on the next article of clothing. Continue until you have "cleaned" all the clothes.

Variation: For an additional challenge, put new stickers on the clothes and ask your child to be the cleaner. Have him ask you "What stain is on your shirt?" and then give him a silly response. You can tell him it is a chocolate stain you got when you jumped into a chocolate river!

⭐77 What Is Behind Picture #1?

Props:
- ❏ 5 pictures
- ❏ Tape
- ❏ Chair

Notes:

Challenge: Asking "What?" questions

Motivation: Anticipation, your child's favorite items/characters, completing a row

How to Play: Print out five pictures of things that your child is highly motivated for (food, trains, animals or pictures of their favorite characters) and number each picture on the back. Arrange the pictures in a row with only their numbers showing. Tape the pictures to a wall within your child's view but out of his reach. Ask your child to sit in a designated question chair and encourage him to ask "What is behind picture #1?" After he has asked the question, jump up and turn the picture around so your child can see what it is. Bring the picture to life in a fun and exaggerated way, for example, pretending to eat the picture of the ice cream or talking in the voice of his favorite character shown on that page. Continue the game until all the pictures have been turned over.

Variation: You can play the same game using "Who?" questions by taping up photographs of people in the family instead.

⟨78⟩ The Funny Face Search

Challenge: Asking "Where?" questions

Motivation: Funny faces

How to Play: Print or draw five pictures of funny faces. Before your child comes into the room, hide the pictures around the room. Ask your child to sit in a chair and tell him that you have hidden pictures of funny faces around the room. Encourage him to ask you "Where is the funny face?" Answer his question, for example, you might say, "Under the table," "In my pocket" or "On the top shelf." Ask your child to go to that spot, find the funny face and give it to you. Once he has given you the picture, try to make the funny face together and then tape the picture to the wall. Keep playing the game until he has found all of the funny faces.

Tip: Since the playroom is usually sparse, you may want to bring in some non-distracting objects to hide things in or underneath.

Props:
- ❏ 5 pictures of funny faces
- ❏ Tape
- ❏ Chair

Notes:

⟨79⟩ What Is in the Box?

Challenge: Asking "What?" questions

Motivation: Anticipation, snacks

How to Play: Fill several opaque storage containers with different snacks and ask your child to sit in a chair. Shake each box separately in front of your child so that he can hear the sound of the food inside. Then encourage him to ask, "What is in the box?" After he has asked the question, open the box, show him what it is and have a snack together! Keep playing until you have eaten all the snacks.

Props:
- ❏ 5 opaque storage containers
- ❏ 5 different snacks
- ❏ Chair

Notes:

⟨80⟩ Quiet . . . Loud!

Challenge: Talking at a socially acceptable volume

Motivation: Silly sentences, guessing

How to Play: Prepare a set of eight cards by writing a silly sentence on each one. For example, you might write "Your feet smell like bananas." Make a separate set of three cards and number them 1 to 3. Tell your child that he will take turns picking one card from the silly sentence pile and one card from the number pile. Explain that the number card will tell him how loudly to read the sentence card. If he picks the number "1," then he will say the sentence in a very quiet whisper. If he picks a "2," he will speak in a normal voice, and if he picks a "3," he will speak in a very loud voice. Model this game by picking a card from each pile and reading the sentence to your

Props:
- ❏ 11 blank card
- ❏ Markers

Notes:

child at the volume indicated on the number card. Once you have read your sentence, ask your child to identify the volume by guessing which number card you got. Take turns picking cards and reading aloud. Continue until you have used all the cards.

Variation: If your child is motivated by competition, keep a score sheet. Points can be earned by guessing the volume number correctly.

Tip: After the game is over, you can continue to use this concept to help your child modulate his voice volume to "2" (normal speaking voice). If your child is talking too quietly or too loudly, simply hold up your fingers to show him which volume he is using. Then help him adjust to a normal volume.

⭐81 Show Me What You Got!

Props:
☐ 4–5 small treasures
☐ A newspaper

Notes:

Challenge: Sharing his observations and discoveries with you

Motivation: Finding special treasures

How to Play: Find or buy 4–5 small motivating treasures for your child (colorful marbles, rocks, stickers, etc.). Tell your child to close his eyes so you can hide a treasure in the room. Once the treasure is hidden, ask your child to open his eyes. Explain to him that while he is looking for the treasure, you will sit quietly in the corner and read the newspaper. When he finds it, ask him to let you know by telling you. Ask your child to begin looking while you start to "read the paper" in the corner. Wait for your child to find it and let you know ("Hey, Dad, I got it!"). When he does, show him how excited you are by celebrating him ("Wow, thanks for telling me!"). Then, ask your child to close his eyes again while you hide the next treasure.

Variation: This game is great played in the bubble bath as well. Once your child is sitting in a nice foamy bath, ask him to close his eyes as you slip a treasure into the bath. Then have him search while you "read the paper."

⭐82 Slow . . . Fast!

Props:
☐ 11 blank cards
☐ Markers

Notes:

Challenge: Talking at a socially acceptable speed

Motivation: Silly sentences, slapstick

How to Play: This game is similar to the volume game above. Prepare a set of eight cards by writing a silly sentence on each one. Create a separate set of three cards and number them 1 to 3. Tell your child that he will take turns picking one card from the silly sentence pile and one card from the number pile. Explain to your child that the number card will tell him how quickly to read the sentence card. If he picks the number "1," then he will say the sentence at a slow speed. If he picks a "2," he will speak at normal speed, and if he picks a "3," he will speak at a fast speed. Model this game by picking a card from each pile and reading the sentence to your child at the speed indicated on the number card. Once you have read your sentence, ask your child to identify the speed by guessing which number card you got. Take turns picking cards and reading aloud. Continue until you have used all the cards.

Variation: If your child is motivated by competition, keep a score sheet. Points can be earned by guessing the speed number correctly.

Tip: After the game is over, you can continue to use the concept to help your child modulate their voice speed to "2" (normal speed). If your child is talking too quickly or too slowly, simply hold up your fingers to show him which speed he is using. Then help him adjust to a normal speed.

Interactive Attention Span

⭐83 Silly Animal Mix-Up

Challenge: Interactive attention span of 9 minutes or longer

Motivation: Animals, silly pictures

How to Play: Collect several pictures of animals and glue each picture to a blank card. Cut each card in half. You will be left with a pile of animal tops and a pile of animal bottoms. Set up two empty boxes in the room. Put all of the animal tops into one box, and all of the animal bottoms into the other box. Take turns with your child picking out one animal top and one animal bottom. Tape each new combination to a piece of paper to create a new silly animal. Help your child choose a name for the mixed up animal. For example, an elephant top matched to a zebra bottom might create an animal called an "elebra!"

Variation: For a further challenge, ask your child to help you tape the two halves together. Then ask for his help in writing the name of the new animal on each card.

Props:
- ❒ 6 pictures of animals
- ❒ 6 blank cards
- ❒ Scissors
- ❒ Glue/tape
- ❒ 2 boxes/bags

Notes:

⭐84 Cube Twister

Props:
- ❏ 2 square cardboard boxes
- ❏ Markers
- ❏ 6 squares of colored paper

Notes:

Challenge: Interactive attention span of 9 minutes or longer

Motivation: Funny positions, anticipation

How to Play: Take a square cardboard box and color each side a different color. Tape six corresponding squares of colored paper onto the floor. Take another square cardboard box and draw a body part on each side. Make sure that you have drawn legs, arms, eyes, mouth, tongue and belly. Throw the color "die" (box) and ask your child to stand on whichever color the box lands on. Then throw the body part "die" (box) and ask your child to do a funny pose with whichever body part it lands on. He might stand on one leg, stick his tongue out or put his arms over his head. See how long he can hold that funny position without moving. Then, take turns!

Tip: If your child is motivated by competition, keep score of who can hold a funny position the longest without moving.

⭐85 All Mixed Up

Props:
- ❏ 5–7 printed pictures
- ❏ Tape

Notes:

Challenge: Interactive attention span of 9 minutes or longer

Motivation: Anticipation, order

How to Play: Choose 5–7 pictures of your child's favorite objects and arrange them in a row. Tape them to a wall within your child's view but out of his reach. Ask your child to look at the pictures carefully and try to remember the order that they are in. Have him close his eyes or turn around and count to five. While he is not looking, mix up the order of the pictures. When your child opens his eyes, ask him to tell you how to put the pictures back in order. Once the pictures are in the original order, mix them up and do it again (or make a new order with new pictures).

Tip: Start with fewer pictures (3–4) and add more pictures according to your child's ability.

⟨86⟩ Pass the Present

Challenge: Interactive attention span of 9 minutes or longer

Motivation: Puzzles, songs

How to Play: Take apart a small jigsaw puzzle (5–7 pieces) and wrap each piece in wrapping paper, as if it was a present. Alternatively, you can cut a favorite picture into 5–7 pieces and do the same. Place the wrapped "presents" into a bag. Sit across from your child and hand him the first present from the bag. Sing one of his favorite songs while you pass the present back and forth to each other. When the song is finished, one of you will be holding the present. Whoever is holding the present can then remove the wrapping paper (and assemble that piece of the puzzle if possible). Continue the game until the puzzle is complete.

Props:
- ❑ 5- to 7-piece puzzle/ printed picture
- ❑ Wrapping paper
- ❑ Tape
- ❑ Bag

Notes:

⟨87⟩ Game Sticks

Challenge: Interactive attention span of 9 minutes or longer

Motivation: Anticipation, a variety of activities that are highly motivating for your child

How to Play: Take five craft sticks and color each stick on one side. Create a poster board listing five fun activities, with each activity corresponding to a number 1–5. For example, "1" might be "Jump across the room from one corner to the next," and "2" might be "Roll on the floor from one end of the room to the next." Tape the poster board list to a wall within your child's view. Model how to hold all the craft sticks in a bunch and then let them fall like pick-up sticks. Count the number of sticks that fall with their colored side up. Explain to your child that the number that you count will be the number activity that you will choose from the list. For example, if you counted three craft sticks, then choose activity number "3." Do the specified activity together with your child. Take turns dropping the sticks and determining the corresponding fun activity. Continue until you have enjoyed every activity on the list!

Props:
- ❑ 5 craft sticks
- ❑ Markers
- ❑ Poster board
- ❑ Tape

Notes:

Tip: To help make sure that the craft sticks do not distract your child, put them on the shelf in between each turn.

⭐88 Let's Go Fishing!

Props:
- ❏ 5–8 blank cards
- ❏ Long stick
- ❏ Markers
- ❏ Magnets
- ❏ String
- ❏ Tape/glue
- ❏ Hula hoop

Notes:

Challenge: Interactive attention span of 9 minutes or longer

Motivation: Your child's specific motivations, catching a fish

How to Play: Create a fishing rod by tying one end of a string to a long stick and the other end to a magnet. Cut 5–8 fish shapes out of blank cards. Glue a magnet to one side of each fish. On the other side, write an activity that your child would like to do (for example, get a massage or play catch, etc.). Make a "fishing pond" by placing a hula hoop on the floor. Place all the fish inside the hula hoop pond with their magnet sides facing up. Hold the fishing rod by the stick, so that the magnet hangs down. Take turns standing outside of the pond and trying to catch a fish with the magnetic fishing rod. Once a fish has been caught, read the activity on the back and do it together. Continue until all the fish have been caught.

Tip: If your child is easily distracted by the fishing rod, put it on the shelf in between turns. If the group of fish on the floor seems distracting, then put down only one fish at a time.

⭐89 A Play of Your Own

Props:
- ❏ 5–7 printed pictures
- ❏ Tape

Notes:

Challenge: Using imagination/role play

Motivation: Stories, plays, props

How to Play: Choose several short story books that involve uncomplicated props, simple plots and have only two roles. You may find these stories or you may choose to write them yourself. For example, the following story involves two friends. "One friend had a banana and the other friend had an umbrella. When both friends got hungry, the friend with the banana shared his snack. Then when it began to rain, the friend with the umbrella shared his umbrella." Read the story to your child and then act it out together. Each of you can play one role using the appropriate prop and then you can switch!

Tip: To get your child especially interested, use a story that involves some of his favorite characters.

⭐90 Animal Charades

Props:
- ❏ 10–12 animal cards
- ❏ box

Notes:

Challenge: Using imagination/role play

Motivation: Cards, pretending

How to Play: Prepare a stack of cards with pictures or names of animals on them. Place the cards into a box. Explain to your child that you will be acting out the animal on the card that you pick and his job is to guess which animal you are! Take turns acting and guessing. Continue until all the cards have been used.

Tip: If your child is motivated by competition, use a scorecard. Points can be earned by guessing the animal correctly. See who wins!

⭐91 I'm a Rock Star!

Challenge: Using imagination/role play

Motivation: Your child's favorite song

How to Play: Bring in one of your child's favorite CDs and a CD player (or an iPhone), a prop to be used as a microphone (like a paper towel tube), and a bag full of costumes. Pick an area of the room to be the designated stage. Tell your child you will take turns picking a song from the CD or iPhone, getting dressed up in a costume, and lip synching the words of the song while he watches as the enthused audience. When the song is over, take a bow and let the other person be the rock star!

Tip: If your child is likely to be controlling or repetitive with the CD/CD player—for example, wanting to play every song from beginning to end—and will not be available to play this game, try performing a rock concert simply by singing one of your favorite songs without the CD/iPhone as your back up.

Props:
❐ CD
❐ CD player (iPhone)
❐ Play microphone
❐ Bag full of costumes

Notes:

⭐92 Magic Rocks

Challenge: Using imagination/role play

Motivation: Crafts, magic, anticipation, silliness

How to Play: Find 4–5 rocks outside and decorate them with markers and glitter. Bring your "magic rocks" into the room and put them onto the shelf. Explain to your child that each rock has its own magic powers. Take down each rock and demonstrate. For example, hold one rock, look into your child's eyes and count to five. Pretend that you have both turned into frogs hopping around the room! Do the same with another rock and watch as it turns you both into flying airplanes. Take turns using each magic rock and see the magic work!

Variation: Take several undecorated rocks and decorate them together with your child. Ask your child to help decide which magic qualities they have. Encourage your child to show his "magic rock collection" to a friend and show her how the magic works!

Props:
❐ 5 rocks
❐ Markers
❐ Glitter

Notes:

⭐93 Pass the Prop

Props:
- ❑ 5–6 household items
- ❑ Bag

Notes:

Challenge: Using imagination/role play

Motivation: Using one object in a variety of funny ways

How to Play: Fill a bag with 5–6 household items and put it on the shelf. The items can be as simple as a fork or a plastic bottle. Take out one prop at a time and pass it back and forth with your child. Explain to your child that each time the prop is passed, the person holding it comes up with an additional way to use the item (and can even act it out). The goal is to find as many ways as possible to use one simple household object. For example, a bowl can be used as a hat, a drum or a funny shoe! See how many ideas you can think of together for each prop. Alternatively, you may want to set a goal for each item (for example, three ideas per object). Continue the game until you have used all the props.

⭐94 Phone a Friend

Props:
- ❑ Small table
- ❑ Table cloth
- ❑ Bag of costumes
- ❑ Play phone
- ❑ Tea set

Notes:

Challenge: Using imagination/role play

Motivation: Different funny characters, anticipation

How to Play: Bring a bag of costumes (include hats, glasses and wigs) into the room. Ask your child to sit in one corner of the room with a play phone and a tea set. Set up a small table covered with a table cloth at the other end of the room. Hide your bag of costumes behind the table. Encourage your child to invite different friends to a tea party by asking him "Do you want to invite Harry to have tea with you? Go ahead and call him!" While your child is making the "phone call," hide behind the table and put on a costume. Once you have been "invited," pop out from behind the table dressed as Harry, and go have tea with your child. Then ask your child to invite a new friend, and repeat the procedure.

Tip: Model the phone call procedure by calling and inviting a doll to the tea party.

⭐95 The "Feel Good" Spinner

Props:
- ❑ Poster board
- ❑ Markers
- ❑ Stickers

Notes:

Challenge: Maintaining physical contact for 60 seconds or more

Motivation: Fun physical activities, completing a pie graph, stickers

How to Play: Using a marker, divide a poster board into four equal squares. On the top right hand corner, write "Right hand." On the top left hand corner, write "Left hand." On the bottom right hand corner, write "Right foot," and on the bottom left hand corner, write "Left foot." Turn the poster into a pie graph by drawing a large circle in the middle of the board. Divide the resulting pie into eight pieces by splitting each pie piece in half. Write a physical activity on each pie piece (for example, "Massage" or "Tickle"). Punch a hole in the middle of the pie and insert a spinner. Explain to your child that the spinner will land on a pie piece and on a larger square. The pie piece will indicate the activity to be done, while the larger square will tell him where on the body the activity will be done. Take turns spinning the spinner and doing the indicated activity to each other. For example, if you land on "Tickle," and on "Right hand," then tickle your child's right hand. See if your child can do each activity for 60 seconds. After you and your child have done each activity, put a sticker on the corresponding pie piece. Continue the game until all the pieces have been covered with a sticker.

Tip: Model this game for your child so that he understands how to play.

Flexibility

 **Basketball Writing**

Challenge: Taking turns during an activity

Motivation: Basketball, words, pictures

How to Play: Set up a basketball hoop (or a bucket) in the room. Tape a big piece of paper to the wall for you to write on. Think of a word, but do not tell it to your child. Draw dashes on the paper to correspond to each letter in your word. Explain to your child that you will fill in one letter in your word every time one of you scores a basket until he can guess the word that you have in mind. Take turns throwing the ball into the basket and filling in a dash with a letter each time one of you scores. Use words that your child will find silly or motivating (for example, the name of their favorite toy or friend). Continue until the word has been completed (or your child guesses it). Then begin again by thinking of a new word or have your child think of the word this time and fill in the dashes each time one of you makes a basket.

Props:
❑ Basketball hoop/ bucket
❑ Ball
❑ Paper
❑ Pen
❑ Tape

Notes:

Variation: If your child cannot read yet, have him guess a picture instead of a word. With each basket scored, you can draw another section of the picture until he can guess what the picture is.

Tip: Use tape to make a line on the floor so that your child knows where to stand when throwing the ball.

⟨97⟩ Making a Book

Props:
- ❏ 5 pieces of paper
- ❏ Stapler
- ❏ 5 pictures from the Internet
- ❏ Glue stick
- ❏ Scissors

Notes:

Challenge: Taking turns during an activity

Motivation: Your child's favorite characters (such as Dora the Explorer or Super Man)

How to Play: Print out five pictures from the Internet of your child's favorite characters or people in the family (whichever is more motivating). Staple five pieces of blank paper together to make a book. Explain to your child that together you will make a book of his/her favorite characters. Tell your child he will be the "cutter" and you will be the "gluer" (or the other way around). For example, he will cut out the first picture that you show him. Once he has cut it out, you will glue it to the paper in the book. Continue this way until your book is complete. When you are done, celebrate your child ("Wow! We did that together. It was so fun taking turns with you. Thank you for being such a good friend.").

Tip: The focus of this game is not fine motor skills but turn-taking. If cutting is hard for your child, ask him to be the gluer. This way he will not be challenged with cutting and taking turns at the same time.

⟨98⟩ Pin the Nose on Elmo

Props:
- ❏ Picture of friend or character
- ❏ Paper
- ❏ Tape
- ❏ Blindfold

Notes:

Challenge: Taking turns during an activity

Motivation: Slapstick, your child's favorite character

How to Play: Draw a picture of your child's favorite character or person missing a body part (for example, draw Elmo without a nose). Tape the picture to the wall. Make a cutout of the missing body part and put double-sided tape on its back. Blindfold and spin your child, and then give him the cutout. Ask him to tape it where it belongs. Take the blindfold off and let him see where he placed it! Then ask your child to blindfold and spin you, and try to do the same. Play this game several times with the same picture or with several different pictures.

Tip: Only put the blindfold on your child if he agrees. If he resists, try putting a big hat on his head that will cover his eyes. You can also ask him to close his eyes—but no peeking!

⭐99 Pass the Picture

Challenge: Taking turns during an activity

Motivation: Drawing a picture together and seeing how it evolves (anticipation)

How to Play: Bring a piece of paper and tell your child that you will be drawing a picture together. He can start by drawing one part of a picture (for example, a house), and then he passes the page to you for you to add something to the picture (like a dog or something specific your child likes). Then you pass the paper back to him, back and forth, until the picture is complete.

Variation: If your child has a hard time knowing when to stop (for example, he is drawing a person and is taking several minutes to draw all the details of that person), you can set a timer for 30 seconds. When the timer beeps, it is time to pass the page to the other person.

Props:
- ❑ Paper
- ❑ Markers

Notes:

⭐100 Yoga!

Challenge: Taking turns during an activity

Motivation: Cards, body movement

How to Play: Bring in a box of yoga cards and pick out one card. Demonstrate the pose that is on the card and then ask your child to copy you. Try to hold the movement together for several seconds and then ask your child to pick the next yoga card. Encourage him to do the pose first and then you try to imitate him. Continue to take turns until you have gone through all the cards.

Recommended Purchase: We recommend Annie Buckley's The Kid's Yoga Deck: 50 Poses and Games at www.chroniclebooks.com or Yogarilla™ Exercises and Activities at www.superduperinc.com.

Props:
- ❑ Yoga cards

Notes:

⭐101 Drawing with Your Feet

Challenge: Taking turns in an activity

Motivation: Trying to draw (and watching you draw) with your feet

How to Play: This is a fun and simple game. Bring in 10 cards with a simple picture drawn on each card, like a star, smiley face, tree, etc. Put a large piece of paper on the floor. Take turns picking a card, showing it to the other person, then putting a marker between your toes and trying to draw the picture on the card. Continue until you have used all the cards.

Variation: To add additional challenge to this game, keep the chosen card a secret. Once you have drawn with your feet, see if the other person can guess what you drew.

Props:
- ❑ 10 blank cards
- ❑ Markers
- ❑ 10 pieces of paper

Notes:

⭐102 My Own Board Game

102

Props:
- ❏ Cardboard
- ❏ Markers
- ❏ 2 pawns
- ❏ Dice
- ❏ 10–12 cards

Notes:

Challenge: Playing games with simple rules

Motivation: Your child's specific motivations

How to Play: Take a big piece of poster board and draw a simple game board on it. You will need a snake path with 20–30 spaces between the beginning and the end. Color at least 10 spaces red (or put a sticker on them) and leave the rest of the spaces empty. The red spaces indicate that the player needs to pick a card when he lands on them. Make a corresponding deck of cards to pick from and write down fun activities on each card. Include some activities that are motivating for your child and some that are challenging for him. For example, you might include both "Act like a monkey" and "Look in your friend's eyes and name all of the people in your family." You will need two small household objects to use as pawns (for example, two different coins or two different colored paper clips) and a small die. Explain to your child that you will roll the die, move the number of spaces indicated and do the activity that you land on. Take turns playing and continue until the first person reaches the end.

Tip: You can reuse the board by simply changing the activity cards.

⭐103 A Story of 3 Words

Props:
- ❏ 18 cards
- ❏ Pen

Notes:

Challenge: Taking turns during an activity, plus imagination and storytelling!

Motivation: Hearing and telling funny stories

How to Play: Create a pile of 18 cards and write one word on each card. Use words that your child may be motivated by and that may make up an interesting story (such as superheroes, animals, etc.). Explain to your child that you will each take turns telling a funny story using the words from the cards each person selects. Begin by going first and picking the first three cards. Then tell a story (as interesting and animated as possible) incorporating all three words. When the story is over ask your child to pick the next three words and to do the same. Continue until you have finished all your cards.

Variation: You can bring in 18 blank cards and come up with the words to write on each card together.

Tip: If your child has a hard time telling a story, ask questions to help him tell more, such as "What happened next?" or "Whom did he meet then?"

This game comes from my nightly ritual of putting my three kids to sleep. Every night before bed, they each give me a word (my three-year-old can't get enough of the word "underwear"!), and then I come up with a story incorporating all three of the words.

 # 104 My Own Memory Game

Challenge: Playing games with simple rules

Motivation: Matching cards of people that your child loves

How to Play: Take or find pictures of five family members or friends who are important to your child. Make two copies of each picture (or use two different pictures of the same person) and shuffle the pictures so that they are randomly ordered. Lay them all face down and take turns trying to find two matching pictures (or two pictures of the same person). Continue to play until you have matched all the pictures. Whoever made the most matches wins!

Props:
- ☐ Pictures of 5 friends/ family (2 each)

Notes:

105 Bingo!

Challenge: Playing games with simple rules

Motivation: Anticipation, winning, your child's specific motivations

How to Play: Take two pieces of paper and draw a grid on each one. The grids should each have 6–8 squares. Select numbers from 1–10 and write a number in each square of the grids. Create a deck of ten cards and number them 1–10. Put the cards in a bag and mix them up. Pick out the first card, read the number out loud, and let your child look on his "bingo board" to see if he has the match. Meanwhile, look on your own board for the match as well. Have several small household items ready to use as "bingo chips" to cover the matching square (paper clips, coins, slips of colored paper, etc.) Continue playing until the first person has covered their whole board and won the game. Play again and ask your child to pick the cards and call out the numbers.

Variation: If your child is especially motivated by something other than numbers (for example, letters, shapes or animals), prepare bingo cards and boards using those instead.

Props:
- ☐ Paper
- ☐ 10 blank cards
- ☐ Small household items
- ☐ Bag

Notes:

⭐106 The Sneeze Spot

Props:
- ❏ Poster board
- ❏ 2 objects as game pieces
- ❏ Die
- ❏ Pen

Notes:

Challenge: Playing games with simple rules, flexibility within the game

Motivation: Seeing you do a funny and exaggerated sneeze

How to Play: Take a large poster board and create a board game by drawing a snake-like path divided into 30–40 spaces, with a beginning, end, and spaces in between. On ten random spaces of the snake path, draw a picture of a nose; these are "sneeze spots." Use two different objects or coins as the game pieces. Take turns rolling the die and moving your piece accordingly. If you land on a sneeze spot, the other person has to make a very loud and funny-sounding sneeze, which "blows" him/her back three spaces. Continue taking turns until one person reaches the end.

Chance games, like chutes and ladders, can be very challenging for children on the autism spectrum. Games involving chance require an incredible amount of flexibility. This chance game was designed after a 9-year-old I work with who just *loves* to hear people sneeze. He even stopped mid-tantrum to hear me sneeze.

⭐107 Fill Your Flower!

Props:
- ❏ Cardboard
- ❏ Scissors
- ❏ Markers
- ❏ 14 bottle caps
- ❏ Blank stickers
- ❏ Velcro®

Notes:

Challenge: Playing games with simple rules

Motivation: Your child's favorite topics, completing a picture

How to Play: Use poster board to draw and cut out two large flowers. The flowers should each have six petals and a circle in their center. Press a small piece of Velcro® onto each petal and onto the center circle. Collect 14 large-sized bottle caps and place a blank sticker inside each cap. Choose two items that your child likes in order to create two different groups of bottle caps. Draw one item that he likes on seven of the caps and a different item that he likes on the other seven (for example, draw apples on seven of the caps and bananas on the other seven). Press a small piece of Velcro® on the back of each bottle cap. Stick a bottle cap from the first group onto the center of the first flower and a bottle cap from the second group onto the center of the second flower. Give your child one flower and take the other one for yourself. Turn the remaining bottle caps over and take turns picking caps. If you choose a cap that matches your flower, then stick it to one of your petals. If it does not match, return it to the pile. Continue playing until the first person has filled all of his flower petals and won the game.

Variation: For an extra challenge, have your bottle caps represent different categories (for example, even numbers and odd numbers).

Note: This game takes some more preparation than the other games, but it is well worth it. Once the game is prepared, you can play it with many variations by simply changing the stickers on the bottle caps.

⟨108⟩ Let's Make a Deal!

Challenge: Making a deal

Motivation: Earning prizes

How to Play: Set up a small "store" in the room by taping some inexpensive prizes or toys to a wall or shelf within your child's view, but out of his reach. Sit behind a table and explain to your child that you are storekeeper of this very unique store. The trick in this store is nothing is bought with money—everything is purchased by making a deal! Ask your child what he would like to buy and then come up with a deal in order for him to get it. For example, you might say, "Oh, so you want the heart sticker? O.K., sing me a song and then you can get it—is that a deal?" If your child agrees, you can ask him to shake hands to "close the deal." Once he has fulfilled his side of the deal, give him the prize that he has earned. Continue playing until he has negotiated for every item that he is interested in.

Variation: Let your child be the storekeeper and negotiate with you!

Props:
- ❏ Table
- ❏ 5–10 simple
- ❏ Inexpensive prizes
- ❏ Tape

Notes:

Creative Closet Prop List

Crafts/art supplies:

☐ Poster board (10)
☐ Envelopes
☐ Blank cards
☐ Pen
☐ Tape
☐ Cardboard
☐ Paper bags
☐ Paper plates (5)
☐ Tape
☐ Crayons/markers
☐ Paper
☐ Scissors
☐ Craft sticks
☐ Stapler
☐ Hole-puncher
☐ Sticky notes
☐ Magazines

Recommended toys/games:

☐ Play money
☐ Beach ball
☐ Bag of costumes (clothes /hats/wigs/glasses/jewelry/funny shoes)
☐ Jump rope
☐ Hula hoop rings (3)
☐ Sequence series cards

Other:

☐ Bag/box (4)
☐ Pictures of 5 friends or family/team members
☐ Pizza box
☐ Large cardboard box
☐ Suitcase
☐ Shoeboxes (3)
☐ Shoes (3 pairs)
☐ Measuring tape
☐ Digital camera
☐ Stopwatch
☐ Apron

Stage Four Games

Communication

⟨109⟩ When, Where, Who?

Challenge: Making himself understood, using context when telling a story

Motivation: Hearing a funny story, anticipation

How to Play: Draw three columns on a poster board and label the first column "When," the next column "Where" and the last column "Who." Label three envelopes similarly (one labeled "When," one labeled "Where" and one labeled "Who"). Take five cards for each envelope, write a phrase on each card that relate to each category and place each card into its corresponding envelope. For example, the cards reading "Today," "On my birthday," "Next year" and "When I was a baby" would be placed into the "When" envelope. Hang the poster board on the wall and ask your child to pick one card from each envelope. Tape each card to its corresponding column on the poster. Use the cards to create a context for a funny story that you will tell your child. For example, if your child picks the cards "When I was a baby," "At the beach" and "Grandma and Grandpa," then you can tell the following story:

> "One time when I was a baby at the beach with Grandma and Grandpa, they decided to take me on a dolphin ride. So they called the dolphin to the shore and we jumped on . . ."

Continue until you have used all the cards to tell your child several different funny stories.

Variation: Take turns picking cards. Have your child use the cards that you have chosen to tell you a story.

Props:
- ❏ Poster board
- ❏ 3 envelopes
- ❏ 15 blank cards
- ❏ Pen
- ❏ Tape

Notes:

⟨110⟩ When, Where, Who? (Advanced)

Challenge: Making himself understood, using context when telling a story

Motivation: Hearing a funny story, anticipation.

How to Play: This game is the same as above, but instead of using cards that correspond to "When," "Where" and "Who," simply ask your child to provide an example of each one.

Write the phrases on the poster board in the appropriate columns and tell another funny story.

Variation: Take turns providing phrases and telling funny stories.

Props:
- ❏ Poster board
- ❏ Pen
- ❏ Tape

Notes:

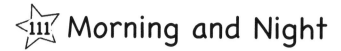 Morning and Night

Props:
- ❏ Poster board
- ❏ Cardboard box
- ❏ Markers
- ❏ Paper
- ❏ Tape

Notes:

Challenge: Answering/asking questions, making statements about past and future events

Motivation: Acting out stories in a funny way, completing a chart

How to Play: Make a chart with a picture of the sun on top and a picture of the moon below it. Draw three blank boxes next to each picture and tape the chart to a wall within your child's view. Take a cardboard box and on three sides make a sun (indicating morning) and on the other three sides make a moon (indicating night). Ask your child to throw the box into the air and see what side it lands on. If the cardboard lands on the "Morning," ask your child "What is something that you did in the morning?" Have your child think of and act out a morning activity (like brushing his teeth) while you try to guess which activity he is portraying. If the card lands on the "Night" side, then ask your child, "What is something that you will do at night?" After you have guessed the activity that he portrayed, fill in the chart. If your child acted out a morning activity, draw a sun in one of the boxes next to the sun. If your child acted out a nighttime activity, draw a moon in one of the squares next to the moon. Take turns acting and guessing until the entire chart has been filled in.

Silly Skits

Props:
- ❏ Props that pertain to each play

Notes:

Challenge: Answering "Why" questions based on what he has just experienced/observed

Motivation: Seeing a funny play, anticipation

How to Play: Before coming into the room, think of 5–10 simple skits that you can act out for your child in fun and dramatic ways. For example, you might pretend to be a man walking across the room to get his book, when he slips on a banana peel and falls. Or, you might pretend to be a woman sitting on a picnic bench eating a snack, when it starts to rain, so she opens her umbrella. Ask your child to sit in a special "Audience Chair" while you put on a show for him. Explain to him that you will be asking him a question after each performance. After each skit, pose a relevant "Why" question, such as "Why did the man fall?" or "Why did the woman open her umbrella?" After your child answers the question, then you can act out the next play. Continue until you have performed all of the skits.

☆113 Safety Cat

Challenge: Answering "why" questions

Motivation: Becoming a superhero, watching you act out interesting scene

How to Play: Give your child a cape and a pair of cat ears (or draw whiskers on his face) and tell him that he is a new superhero named "Safety Cat." Tell your child that his job is to watch you carefully. If it looks like you may do something dangerous, he is to jump in and stop you by saying "Stop—Safety Cat to the rescue!" Then, begin to act out a scene in which you are about to do something dangerous, narrating out loud. For example, you can say, "Wow, what a busy street! I think I am going to cross this street while I am reading this very interesting book." Then pretend to begin crossing a street while reading a book. See if your child comes in to say "Stop—Safety Cat to the rescue!" If he does not, prompt him that this is the time to come and save you. Once he says "stop," ask him why you should stop so that he can explain to you what is dangerous about what you were just about to do. After he explains, give your child a big thank you, such as, "Safety Cat, you saved my life. Thank you!" You can repeat this game over and over with a variety of scenes, such as pretending to run across the room with a sharp knife, pretending to play with matches, etc.

Tip: You can play this game with another person serving as Safety Cat's assistant, helping your child know when to jump in to rescue you. You can also use this game as a way to address very specific safety issues you are trying to teach your child about.

This is a game I made up when I was working with an 8-year-old girl who was having a hard time understanding "Why?" questions. It was a blast, and she really got the idea of how to answer "Why?" questions.

Prop:
☐ A cape and cat ears or face paints to draw whiskers

Notes:

☆114 Cliff Hanger

Challenge: Asking "Why" questions

Motivation: Anticipation, telling a funny story in an animated way

How to Play: Before going into the room, compose 3–5 stories similar to the one described below. Explain to your child that you are going to tell him a very interesting story, but that you will need his participation. Tell him that you will stop occasionally and motion for him to ask a "Why" question (like pointing or winking) in order to keep the story going. A sample story is below:

> "Once there was a man who was freezing cold (stop, motion to your child to ask, 'Why was he freezing cold?' and then continue) because it was the middle of the winter but he was wearing a bathing suit (stop,

Props:
☐ Paper
☐ Pen

Notes:

motion to your child to ask, 'Why was he in his bathing suit?' and then continue) because all of his winter clothes were in the laundry. He decided to talk a walk down the street, when he suddenly burst out laughing (stop, motion to your child to ask, 'Why did he laugh?' and then continue) because he saw a woman walking toward him in her bathing suit too . . . "

Continue until you have told all of the stories that you prepared.

Variation: To make the game even sillier, freeze your body in a funny position every time you pause for the "Why" question, and only unfreeze once your child has asked the question.

Tip: Try modeling this game with another team member first so that your child can see exactly how to play.

⟨115⟩ The Amazing World of Nature

Props:

Props:
- ☐ 5–10 science pictures
- ☐ Tape
- ☐ Paper
- ☐ Stapler

Notes:

Challenge: Asking "Why" questions

Motivation: Anticipation, learning about interesting pictures

How to Play: Choose 5–10 science pictures (from magazines or from the Internet). Place the pictures on the shelf. Explain to your child that you will show him some very interesting pictures, but that you will need his participation. Tell him that you will bring down each picture, one at a time, and explain what the picture is showing, and that you will then motion to him to ask a "Why" question to find out more. For example, show your child a picture of a chameleon and explain that the chameleon changes colors depending on its environment. Pause and motion to your child to ask "Why?" Once he has asked the question, continue your explanation by saying that it changes color in order to camouflage and defend itself. Then, show your child the next picture and repeat this process until you have discussed each picture.

Variation: After you have finished discussing each picture, tape it to a piece of paper and write down the information you have learned about it. Staple the pictures together and make your own science book.

Tip: When choosing pictures pick a topic that is especially motivating for your child.

☆116 Our Amazing Bodies

Challenge: Asking "Why" questions

Motivation: Anticipation, learning about interesting pictures

How to Play: Choose 5–10 pictures of the human body (from magazines or from the Internet). Place the pictures on the shelf. Explain to your child that you will show him some very interesting pictures, but that you will need his participation. Tell him that you will explain what the picture is showing, and that you will then motion to him to ask a "Why" question to find out more. For example, show your child a picture of an eye with eyelashes. Explain that humans have eyelashes on the top and lower lids of their eyes. Pause and motion to your child to ask "Why?" Once he has asked the question, continue your explanation by saying that eyelashes protect the eyes by catching small particles of dust and dirt. Then, show your child the next picture and repeat this process until you have discussed each picture.

Variation: After you have finished discussing each picture, tape it to a piece of paper and write down the information you have learned about it. Staple the pictures together and make your own body book.

Props:
- ☐ 5–10 pictures of the body
- ☐ Tape
- ☐ Paper
- ☐ Stapler

Notes:

☆117 Your Own Fashion Show

Challenge: Answering simple questions requiring his opinion within the answer

Motivation: Dressing you up, watching a fashion show

How to Play: Prepare four bags of costumes for use in a "fashion show." Fill one of the bags with 4 hats, one with 4 shirts, one with 4 skirts/pants and one with 4 pieces of jewelry. Take out the contents of one bag and ask your child, "Which hat/shirt/pants/jewelry do you like?" Put on the item that your child selected and put the rest of the items back in the bag and up on the shelf. Repeat this process with each bag of costumes. Once you are dressed, ask your child to sit down so he can watch his very own fashion show. Your child might love it if you walk down a pretend runway in a very dramatic way! When you are done, repeat the same process and let your child choose his next outfit for you to put on. Continue until all the clothing items have been used.

Props:
- ☐ 4 bags
- ☐ 4 hats
- ☐ 4 shirts
- ☐ 4 pieces of jewelry
- ☐ 4 skirts/pants

Notes:

☆118 The Big Spin

Props:

❏ 10 pieces of paper
❏ Pen

Notes:

Challenge: Answering simple questions requiring his opinion within the answer

Motivation: Anticipation (spinning and seeing where he lands)

How to Play: Take 10 pieces of paper, and on the back of each piece write a personal question for your child to answer (e.g., "What game do you like to play and why?" "What are the names of three of your friends?" "What is your favorite season and why?"). Adjust the level of questions according to your child's level. Put the cards in a big circle and ask your child to stand in the middle. Ask your child to close his eyes and spin around (to the count of three) with his arm extended and his finger pointed. Once he gets to three, he can open his eyes and see which piece of paper he is most closely pointing to. Then he can read and answer the question on that paper. After he has answered the question, remove that paper from the circle. Continue until all the pieces of paper have been removed from the circle.

Variation: You can play this game again, this time with your child making up the questions and writing them on the back of 10 pieces of paper. Then you can spin and answer the questions your child created for you.

☆119 Make Your Own Menu

Props:

❏ 5 paper plates
❏ Food pictures
❏ Tape

Notes:

Challenge: Answering simple questions requiring his opinion within the answer

Motivation: Food, making up menus

How to Play: Choose 15 assorted pictures of different foods (from magazines or from the Internet). Include five pictures each of vegetables, main dishes and desserts. Tape the vegetable pictures to one wall of the playroom, the main dish pictures to a second wall and the dessert pictures to a third wall. Bring in five paper plates and put one on the table and the remaining four on the shelf. Ask your child to choose a vegetable picture that he would like to "eat" and have him tape it to the paper plate. Then ask your child which main dish picture that he thinks would go well with that vegetable and tape that picture to the plate. Finish off the "meal" by asking him which dessert would go well with the meal he has created so far and tape it to the plate. Continue until your child has made five different meal combinations on five different plates. When you are done with the menu, play a restaurant game in which your child serves you the different pretend meals that he has planned.

⟨120⟩ Making Scenery

Challenge: Answering simple questions requiring his opinion within the answer

Motivation: Making scenery, watching plays

How to Play: Take three large pieces of paper or poster board and use a black marker to draw a different scene on each one. For example, you might draw a beach, a castle and a snowy day. Create two stick characters by drawing simple figures on paper, cutting them out and stapling them to craft sticks. Put the stick characters on a shelf together with crayons or markers. Tape one poster board scene to the wall and ask your child, "Which color should we use to make the trees/castle?" Use the color that he has chosen to color in that part of the scenery. Put the crayon/marker back on the shelf and ask your child to choose a color for the next part of the scenery. Continue until the poster board scene is complete. Take out the stick characters and perform a short play for your child. Use the backdrop that you created together as the scenery! Continue this process with the other scenes you have prepared.

Variation: For an additional challenge, ask your child to choose a name for each character. You can also leave one poster board blank and ask him, "What kind of scene should we draw for the next play?" Use his answer in order to create the next scene.

Props:
- ❑ 3 large pieces of paper/poster board
- ❑ Tape
- ❑ Crayons/markers
- ❑ Paper
- ❑ Scissors
- ❑ Craft sticks
- ❑ Stapler

Notes:

⟨121⟩ Album of Friends

Challenge: Showing interest in others (asking simple questions about another person)

Motivation: Pictures, friends, making a book

How to Play: Collect five pictures of your child's friends, family members or team members, and put them onto the shelf. Create a book consisting of 5–7 empty pages stapled together, with the cover titled "An Album of My Friends." On the bottom of each page, help your child write 2–3 personal questions to ask each person. Make sure to leave space on each page for the answers. Assist your child in interviewing each person (either by phone or in person). Tape a picture of the friend at the top of each page and use the interview answers to fill in the bottom of the page.

Tip: If you are going to conduct the interviews by phone, make arrangements ahead of time. You want to be sure that the interviewee will be available when you will be doing your project.

Props:
- ❑ 5–10 pictures of friends/family/team members
- ❑ Tape
- ❑ Paper
- ❑ Stapler
- ❑ Pen
- ❑ Phone

Notes:

 **Blow Maze**

Props:
☐ Ping-pong ball
☐ Masking tape
☐ 3–6 index cards

Notes:

Challenge: Answering simple questions requiring his opinion within the answer

Motivation: Going through a maze

How to Play: Create a room-sized maze using masking tape to mark the edges of the path. At 4–5 selected points in the maze place a card (face down) with a question for your child that requires his opinion, like "Whom do you like to play with and why?" Give your child a ping-pong ball and a straw. Ask him to start at the beginning of the maze and get down on the ground and blow the ball through the maze. When he gets to a card spot, tell him to stop and read the question. Wait for his answer, and then continue until he reaches the end of the maze.

Variation: You can add cards with other motivators for your child to increase his level of interest, like "get a spin/tickle."

Tip: You may need to tell your child to take a break at some point so he does not get too light-headed. Also, you can take turns and do the maze yourself. You can even keep track of your time to see if you can do it faster the next time!

123 Word Search

Props:
☐ Paper
☐ Pen

Notes:

Challenge: Showing interest in others (asking simple questions about another person)

Motivation: Searching for words, reading

How to Play: Make up a list of five personal questions for your child to ask you. For example, you might choose "What color are your eyes?," "What do you like to eat for breakfast?" and "What is the name of one of your friends?" Prepare a word search grid using the answers you will be giving. Hide your answers among all the other letters. For example:

"What color are your eyes?" Blue

"What do you like to eat for breakfast?" Eggs

"What is the name of one of your friends?" Sam

x z b e s a m r

y a l y n f d r

j w u y k f s f l

f h e g g s o j

Give your child the list of questions that you prepared. After your child asks you each question and receives each answer from you, he can find the answer in the word search grid. Continue until your child has found and circled all the answers.

 124 How Do You Measure Up?

Challenge: Showing interest in others

Motivation: Using a measuring tape, numbers and compiling "data"

How to Play: Before you go into the room, make a simple book by stapling five pieces of paper together. On the cover write "How do you measure up?" On each page write "Name of person being measured" and then list five areas to measure, such as height, length of foot, width of smile, length of face, etc. Encourage your child to begin by measuring you. He can write your name on the top of the first page (or you can write for him). Then, using a measuring tape, he can measure you and list each measurement on your page. Your child can do this same activity with other members of your family and team.

Variation: At the end, you can determine who is the tallest, who has the widest smile, etc., and your child can make and give awards to each one of these people.

Props:
☐ Paper
☐ Stapler
☐ Pencil
☐ Measuring tape

Notes:

125 Secret Code

Challenge: Showing interest in others (asking simple questions about another person)

Motivation: Decoding letters, mystery

How to Play: Make up a list of five personal questions for your child to ask you. Create an alphabet code (with each letter represented by a symbol) and copy it onto a poster board. Prepare five cards with your answers to each personal question written in code. Make a line above each symbol so that your child can write the corresponding letter. Give your child the question list that you prepared and after your child asks you each question, hand him the answer card written in code. Ask him to decode the answer using the alphabet code. Once he has decoded and discovered the answer, have him ask you the next question. Continue until your child has asked you all of the questions and decoded all of the cards.

Props:
☐ Paper
☐ Pen
☐ 5–10 blank cards
☐ Poster board

Notes:

⟨126⟩ Friendly Bus Driver

Props:
- ❏ Large cardboard box
- ❏ Markers
- ❏ Scissors
- ❏ Rope
- ❏ Chair
- ❏ Blank card

Notes:

Challenge: Having conversations that consist of 3–5 loops or more

Motivation: Getting a ride in a box, going to imaginary places

How to Play: Find a large cardboard box and draw wheels and windows on the outside in order to make it look like a bus. Cut a hole on one side of the box and tie a rope through it so you can pull your child on the "bus." Explain to your child that you will be the bus driver. Offer to take him wherever he would like to go and hand him a "bus ticket" (you can use a blank card). Ask your child to sit down at the "bus stop" (a designated chair) and wait for the bus to arrive. Drive the bus around by pulling the rope until you arrive at the bus stop. Then begin a short conversation with your child of 3–5 loops. A sample conversation appears below.

> You: Good morning.
>
> Child: Good Morning.
>
> You: How are you today?
>
> Child: Fine.
>
> You: Where would you like to go today?
>
> Child: To the beach.
>
> You: Excellent! Do you have a bus ticket?
>
> Child: Yes.

Take your child's bus card and give him a ride. Pretend to arrive at the beach and take several minutes to play at the beach together. Then drive your child back to the bus stop and begin the game again, but with a different destination. Play this several times, bringing your child to a new place each time.

Variation: Instead of using a box, you can set up a small row of chairs as the bus. Let the bus driver sit in the front seat. This way your child can be the driver too (since you are likely too heavy to pull in a box)!

Tip: If your child finds it difficult to keep the conversation going by responding to your questions/comments, help him by whispering an appropriate response. If he can read, you can even write a script for him to use. Try using the script for the first couple of rounds of the game and then you can try to phase it out over time. Ultimately, the goal is to have him respond on his own.

⭐127 Superhero Interview

Challenge: Showing interest in others (asking simple questions about another person)

Motivation: Your child's favorite superheroes or characters

How to Play: Set up two chairs across from each other and ask your child to sit in one of the chairs. Tell your child that today he gets to meet some special guests who will be coming to his very own playroom! He has the opportunity to ask these guests anything he would like to find out about them. Leave the room and put on a superhero costume. Make a dramatic entrance (like sweeping your cape as you fly in), sit down, and ask your child what he would like to know. If your child has a hard time coming up with a question, you can prompt him by saying, "Would you like to know my name or my super power? Then ask!" Once your child has asked several questions, you can leave the room, get dressed as another superhero, and repeat the interview process several times.

Tips: If it is especially challenging for your child to come up with questions, you can come up with a list of questions together before the superheroes come in. Then he can ask what you have rehearsed or written down together.

Variation: If your child enjoys writing or compiling information, you can make up interview sheets ahead of time, and your child can write down the answers as he hears them.

Props:
- ☐ Costumes for several superheros or funny characters
- ☐ 2 chairs

Notes:

⭐128 Pizza Shop

Challenge: Having conversations that consist of 3–5 loops or more

Motivation: Eating/buying/selling pretend pizza

How to Play: Cut a piece of cardboard into three circles (one small, one medium and one large) and decorate them into pizzas (without toppings). Place the circles onto a small table in the room. Draw and cut out different paper "toppings" and tape them to the wall directly behind the table. Put on an apron and stand behind the table. Tell your child that you are the owner of a new pizza shop and that he is the customer. Then, begin a short conversation with your child of 3–5 loops. A sample conversation appears below.

> You: Hello, sir.
>
> Child: Hello.
>
> You: Would you like a pizza today?
>
> Child: Yes.
>
> You: Great! Would you like a small, medium or large pizza?

Props:
- ☐ Cardboard
- ☐ Markers
- ☐ Paper
- ☐ Tape
- ☐ Apron
- ☐ Play money (optional)
- ☐ Pizza box (optional)

Notes:

Child: Large.

You: O.K., coming right up! Would you like any toppings? We have mushrooms, peppers or olives.

Child: Olives—I love olives.

(Put olives on your child's pizza.)

You: Here you go, sir. That will be 30 dollars.

(Your child can pay you with play or imaginary money.)

Child: Here you go. Thank you! Bye!

You: Bye!

Encourage your child to "eat" his pretend pizza. Then, continue the game by asking your child to be a new customer.

Variation: Switch roles with your child and allow him to be the pizza owner and you can be the customer.

Tip: If your child finds it difficult to keep the conversation going by responding to your questions/comments, help him by whispering an appropriate response. If he can read, you can even write a script for him to use. Try using the script for the first couple of rounds of the game and then you can try to phase it out over time. Ultimately, the goal is to have him respond on his own.

⭐129 Shoe Store

Props:
- ❏ Three pairs of funny shoes
- ❏ Three shoeboxes
- ❏ Table
- ❏ Tape measure
- ❏ Play money (optional)

Notes:

Challenge: Having conversations that consist of 3–5 loops or more

Motivation: Trying on different shoes, using a tape measure, anticipation

How to Play: Choose three pairs of shoes and put each pair into a shoebox. Put the shoeboxes onto a shelf, and sit behind a small table. Tell your child that you have set up a shoe store and that you would be happy to sell him shoes. Then, begin a short conversation with your child of 3–5 loops. A sample conversation appears below.

You: Hello! Welcome to the best shoe store in town!

Child: Thank you.

You: Can I measure your foot so that we can find the shoes that will fit you best?

Child: Yes. My feet are very big.

You: Great! (Use a tape measure to measure your child's foot.) Let's see. . . . You are a size 6. Now, what kind of shoe would you like? (You can narrow his choice by asking, "Would you like a running shoe or a fancy shoe?")

Child: Big, bouncy ones.

You: O.K., I have the perfect pair! (Take down one shoebox and put the shoes onto your child's feet.) Take a peek in the mirror—how do they look?

Child: Funny! I look like a clown.

You: Would you like to buy them?

Child: Yes.

You: O.K., that will be $30. (Your child can pay you with play or imaginary money)

Child: Here you go. Thank you! Bye!

You: Bye!

Continue playing until your child has bought all three pairs of shoes.

Variation: Switch roles with your child and allow him to be the shoe store owner. You may have to take the shoeboxes off the shelf so that your child can reach them.

Tip: If your child finds it difficult to keep the conversation going by responding to your questions/comments, help him by whispering an appropriate response. If he can read, you can even write a script for him to use. Try using the script for the first couple of rounds of the game and then you can try to phase it out over time. Ultimately, the goal is to have him respond on his own.

⟨130⟩ Spell Master

Challenge: Speaking using nouns, verbs, prepositions, adjectives, pronouns, conjunctions and articles

Motivation: Words, spelling, reading, being the "master"

Props:
- ☐ Markers
- ☐ Paper
- ☐ Tape

Notes:

How to Play: Choose 3–4 words that your child knows how to spell. Write each letter of each word on a separate slip of paper (for example, c-l-o-w-n for the word "clown"). Collect the letters that make up the first word. Tape the letters randomly onto a wall within your child's view but out of his reach. Tell your child that you heard he was a "spell master" and that you need some help spelling the word "clown." Ask him to tell you how to rearrange the letters. Encourage your child to describe exactly where to put each letter and continue until the word is spelled correctly. Keep playing until all the words have been rearranged into their correct spellings.

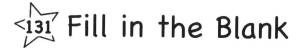 131 Fill in the Blank

Props:
- ☐ 30 cards
- ☐ Red, blue, green markers
- ☐ Poster board
- ☐ Tape

Notes:

Challenge: Speaking in a complete sentence (using noun, verb, and adjective)

Motivation: Watching you act out funny sentences

How to Play: Create a space for a sentence on a poster board by writing the word "The" and then draw a big red square (for the adjective), a big blue square (for the noun), and a big green square (for the verb). Make a stack of 5–10 cards, with an adjective written on one side (such as "tired," "sad," "fat," "old," etc.) and a red star on the other side. Make a another stack of 5–10 cards, with a noun written on one side (such as a person or animal that you can act out) and a blue star on the other side. Make a third stack of 5–10 cards, with a verb written on one side (such as "sleeps," "dances," "eats," "cries," etc.) and a green star on the other side. Ask your child to pick a card with a red star and tape it in the red square, then a card with a blue star for the blue square, and finally a card with a green star for the green square. Then ask your child to read the whole sentence, such as "The sad baby dances!" If your child does not read, you can read it for him and he can repeat after you. Finally, act out the sentence in a silly way for your child. Continue by asking your child to select new cards to make the next funny sentence until you have used up all the cards.

Variation: You can also take turns with your child—you can pick the cards and he can act out the funny sentences.

Tip: Don't throw out the cards when you are done! This game can be played again and again with you or other team or family members. And you can always add new cards.

132 Get Me to My Carrot!

Props:
- ☐ Household objects for an obstacle course (chair, rope, small table and several hula-hoops)
- ☐ Costumes for a rabbit
- ☐ Paper
- ☐ Tape

Notes:

Challenge: Speaking using nouns, verbs, prepositions, adjectives, pronouns, conjunctions and articles

Motivation: Control, funny costumes, slapstick

How to Play: Create a simple obstacle course in the room. For example, the course might consist of a chair, three hula-hoops, a rope to walk along and a table to crawl under. Dress up as a rabbit (with ears and a tail) and tape a picture of a carrot to the wall at the end of the obstacle course. Tell your child that you are a very hungry rabbit but that you cannot figure out how to get to your carrot. Ask your child to verbally direct you there (for example, "Hop in the hoop, crawl under the table and walk across the rope . . ."). Follow your child's directions until you get to your carrot. When you get to the carrot, gobble it up enthusiastically!

Variation: Play again, but change the obstacle course. Alternatively, dress up as a different animal—pretend you are a monkey trying get to his banana or an elephant looking for his peanuts.

Tip: If your child finds it challenging to direct you, give him some examples of things he can say to get you through each section of the course.

⟨133⟩ The Alien Game

Challenge: Speaking using nouns, verbs, prepositions, adjectives, pronouns, conjunctions and articles

Motivation: Watching you make silly mistakes

How to Play: Dress up in a funny costume and tell your child that you are an alien from a different planet and need to learn how to do things here on Earth. Bring in a toothbrush, a tube of toothpaste, an empty bowl, and a cup of water. Ask your child to teach you how to brush your teeth. As your child begins to explain, take his direction *very literally.* For example, if he says, "Put the toothpaste on the toothbrush," then take the toothpaste tube and simply place it on the tooth brush. Seeing you do things so literally will both be funny and help your child be more specific ("Twist the top until it comes off, squeeze the toothpaste onto the brush part of the tooth brush," etc.). Do only *exactly* what your child tells you to do until he has directed you to brush your teeth correctly.

Variation: You can be an alien each day of the week and ask your child to teach you how to get dressed, make a sandwich, or eat a bowl of cereal!

All three of my kids beg me to play this game with them; it cracks them up each time! This is a personal favorite…

Props:
- ❏ Funny costume
- ❏ Toothbrush
- ❏ Toothpaste
- ❏ Bowl
- ❏ Cup (or any object related to activity child is going to instruct you to do)

Notes:

⟨134⟩ Body Language Charades

Challenge: Understanding and using basic social cues (facial expressions, tone of voice and body language)

Motivation: Exaggerated body movements, acting out different scenarios, anticipation, guessing

How to Play: Prepare 7–10 cards with examples of body language written on them. For example, the cards might say "Shrug your shoulders," "Cross your arms with an angry look on your face," or "Jump up and down with an excited expression on your face." Put the cards into a box or bag and mix them up. Pick a card, read the directions and act out what the card says. Then, ask your child to guess what feeling you are depicting through your body language. Continue playing until you have gone through all of the cards.

Variation: Take turns picking cards so that your child has a chance to act out the body language scenarios. If he doesn't read, prepare cards with pictures.

Props:
- ❏ 7–10 cards
- ❏ Pen/markers
- ❏ Box/bag

Notes:

⭐135 Lights, Camera, Action!

Props:
- ❑ A short, two-character play
- ❑ Appropriate props/ costumes

Notes:

Challenge: Understanding and using basic social cues (facial expressions, tone of voice and body language)

Motivation: Putting on a play

How to Play: Select a two-character play (could be from a book, the Internet or one you write yourself). For example, you could create a play about one friend who is upset and another friend who plans a party to help cheer him up. Tell your child that you and he will be acting out a play together. Read him the play, pick your roles, and choose any appropriate props or costumes. Rehearse the play together, encouraging your child to use his voice to convey his character's feelings. Practice the play several times together until your child has used his voice in a dramatic way to express his character's feelings. Then, you can create invitations, invite family members, and put on a play for everybody—and don't forget the popcorn!

⭐136 Make a Face!

Props:
- ❑ 7–10 cards
- ❑ Markers
- ❑ Digital camera
- ❑ Box/bag

Notes:

Challenge: Understanding and using basic social cues (facial expressions, tone of voice and body language)

Motivation: Using a digital camera, acting

How to Play: Prepare 5–7 cards with different feelings written on them. For example, you might write "Surprised," "Excited," "Tired," and "Proud." Put the cards into a box or bag and mix them up. Pick a card, read it out loud and ask your child to make the appropriate facial expression. Use a digital camera to snap pictures of your child as he acts out the feelings. Continue playing until your child has gone through all of the cards.

Later, print out the pictures and label each one with the feeling it is depicting. These "Feeling cards" can be used for the How Might You Feel? game below.

‹137› How Might You Feel?

Challenge: Understanding and using basic social cues (facial expressions, tone of voice and body language)

Motivation: Anticipation, matching, completing a poster, watching you act

How to Play: This game uses the "Feeling cards" from the Make a face! game above.

Tape the "Feeling cards" to the wall. Draw a line down the center of a poster board and hang it next to the cards. One the top left side of the poster, write "Situation." On the top of the right side of the poster, write "Feeling." Prepare "situation cards" by writing scenarios on several blank cards. The scenarios that you choose should be ones that elicit the feelings found on the "Feeling cards." For example, the scenario "You see a friend you have not seen in a long time" might elicit "Surprised" or "Excited." Put the "Situation cards" into a box or bag and mix them up. Pick a card, read the scenario and tape it onto the poster under the "Situation" column. Then, ask your child to pick a corresponding "Feeling card" and tape it onto the poster under the "Feeling" column. After you have read each scenario to your child and he has picked the matching feeling card, act out the scenario in a dramatic way. Continue playing until all the cards have been taped to the poster.

Props:
- ❑ Poster board
- ❑ Markers
- ❑ Tape
- ❑ "Feeling cards"
- ❑ "Situation cards"

Notes:

‹138› Memory with Feelings

Challenge: Understanding and using basic social cues (facial expressions, tone of voice and body language)

Motivation: Anticipation, matching

How to Play: This game uses the "Feeling cards" from the Make a Face! game and the "Situation cards" from the How Might You Feel? game.

Draw one symbol on the back of all the "Feeling cards" and a different symbol on the back of all the "Situation cards" to distinguish them from each other. Turn all of the cards face down. Take turns picking two cards (one from each category) and trying to match a "Feeling card" to a corresponding "Situation card." For example, "You come home to find that all your friends have planned a surprise party for you" would match "Surprised." If the "Feeling card" and "Situation card" are not related, then put the cards back in the pile face down. Continue playing until all of the cards have been matched. The person with the most cards at the end of the game is the winner!

Props:
- ❑ Markers
- ❑ "Feeling cards"
- ❑ "Situation cards"

Notes:

⟨139⟩ Lies or Truth?

Props:
- ☐ 8 blank cards
- ☐ 2 boxes/bags

Notes:

Challenge: Understanding and using basic social cues (facial expressions, tone of voice and body language)

Motivation: Telling stories, guessing, anticipation

How to Play: This game is best played with three people.

Take five cards and write a conversation topic on each one. For example, the topics might include "Birthday party," "Trip to the doctor," "Day at the beach" or "Camping." Put the cards into a "Topic" bag (or box) and mix them up. Take an additional three cards to put into a "Truth/Lies" bag. Write the word "Truth" on two of the cards and the word "Lies" on the third card. Take one card out of the "Topic" bag and read it out loud to the two players. Explain that they will need to tell a story about this topic in a few minutes. Have each player pick a card from the "Truth/Lies" bag. Explain that they will read the card to themselves and then put it back into the bag—without telling anyone else what it said. Depending on whether they chose a "Truth" or "Lies" card, they will tell a true story or a fictitious story on the given topic. After each player has told his story, the other two people need to guess whether it was the "Truth" or "Lies." After each round, pick a new topic card and have the players pick new cards from the "Truth/"Lies" bag.

Variation: If your child does not read yet, create different "Truth/"Lie" cards. Make an "x" on one of the cards and leave the other two cards blank. The card with the "x" is equivalent to a "Lies" card and the blank cards are "Truth" cards.

Tip: The goal of this game is to help identify facial expression and social cues. You can help facilitate this by pointing out that certain facial expressions and/or lack of eye contact are good indicators that someone is not telling the truth.

⟨140⟩ The Conversation Pass

Props:
- ☐ 5–10 cards
- ☐ Pen
- ☐ Beach ball
- ☐ Paper (optional)

Notes:

Challenge: Taking turns talking and listening

Motivation: Playing ball

How to Play: Prepare a stack of cards with different conversation topics written on them (or pictures if your child does not yet read). Choose topics that your child is familiar with (for example, a family trip, fun things to do at the beach, a time when you were sick, etc.). Bring a beach ball into the room and hold it on your lap. Tell your child that the person holding the ball will speak while the other person listens. Pick a conversation card, read it aloud and begin to talk about that topic while your child listens. Then, throw the ball to him. When he catches it, he can begin telling his own story about that topic. When he is done, it is his turn to pick a new conversation card. This time, you will need to be ready to catch the ball and continue the conversation. Take turns initiating conversation until you have gone through all the conversation cards.

Variation: If your child likes competition, keep score on paper. You can each start with 10 points and then lose a point if you speak while the other person is holding the ball. The person with the most points at the end is the winner!

 **Click-Flash-Share!**

Challenge: Taking turns talking and listening

Motivation: Using a camera

How to Play: Tell your child that you are going to go on a short walk in the neighborhood and that you will each take pictures of things you find interesting or pretty along the way. You can either share a camera or bring along one for each of you. Take your walk together and snap pictures of whatever seems interesting to you. When you get back, take turns showing each other each the pictures you took and explaining to the other person what each one is and why you took a picture of it.

Variation: This activity can be done many times in different environments, like around the house, at the store, visiting the zoo, etc.

Props:
- ☐ 1–2 digital cameras

Notes:

142 Time's Up!

Challenge: Taking turns talking and listening

Motivation: Talking quickly, slapstick

How to Play: Put a stopwatch/timer onto the shelf. Prepare 5–7 cards with different conversation topics written on them. Choose topics that your child is familiar with (for example, a family trip, fun things to do at the beach, a time when you were sick, etc.). If your child cannot read, draw a picture on each card instead. Set the timer for 30 seconds and pick a card. Talk about the topic until the timer beeps. Then, set the timer again and have your child do the same with the chosen topic. Continue playing until you have used all the cards.

Variation: If your child likes competition, you can each start with 10 points. You lose a point by either speaking after the timer beeps or by stopping before the timer beeps. The person with the most points at the end of the game wins!

Props:
- ☐ 5–7 cards
- ☐ Stopwatch/timer
- ☐ Pen

Notes:

⟨143⟩ Conversation Starter

Props:

☐ 2 pieces of cardboard
☐ Sticky notes
☐ Pen
☐ Paper
☐ Tape

Notes:

Challenge: Initiating/starting a conversation

Motivation: Anticipation, funny stories

How to Play: Use cardboard to create two game boards. Make sure that each board has four spaces on it. Draw or tape a picture onto each space. Choose items that are familiar and interesting to your child (for example, a birthday cake, a dog, and an umbrella). Cover each picture with a sticky note. Uncover a picture on your board and use the picture as a conversation starter for a funny story. For example, if you uncover a picture of an umbrella, you might say, "One day I went outside in the rain with my umbrella and took a walk when I stepped in a huge puddle and got my socks soaking wet." Encourage your child to continue the conversation with a question, related statement or story. Then, have your child uncover one of the cards on his board and use it to start a new conversation. Continue until each person has revealed all his pictures on his board.

Interactive Attention Span

⟨144⟩ Lip Reading

Props:

☐ 20 cards
☐ Markers
☐ Box/bag
☐ Paper (optional)

Notes:

Challenge: Interactive attention span of 20 minutes or longer

Motivation: Anticipation

How to Play: Prepare a stack of approximately 20 cards with a word written on each one. If your child cannot read yet, prepare cards with pictures on them instead. Mix up the cards and put them into a bag or box. Pick a card but do not show your child the word written on it. "Mouth" the word without using your voice and see if your child can read your lips. If he can, ask him to tell you what you said!

Variation: If your child likes competition, keep score on paper. For example, allow 2–3 chances to guess a word and 1 point for each correct guess. The first person to get 10 points is the winner!

⭐145 The Surprise Sneeze

Challenge: Interactive attention span of 20 minutes or longer

Motivation: Watching you make an exaggerated sneeze, anticipation

How to Play: Take 10 cards and write a fun activity on seven of the cards, such as "Hop across the room on two feet" or "Hold hands and spin until you fall down," etc. On the remaining three cards draw a picture of a nose; these are "Surprise Sneeze" cards. Ask your child to pick a card from the hat and then act out the activity written on it. If he picks the "Surprise Sneeze" card, then you act out a very dramatic and hysterical sneeze—it could even include falling flat on the floor! Continue until your child has picked all the cards and done all the activities.

Props:
- ☐ 10 cards
- ☐ Pen

Notes:

⭐146 What's Different about Me?

Challenge: Interactive attention span of 20 minutes or longer

Motivation: Anticipation, costumes

How to Play: Bring a bag of simple costumes (including scarves, socks, jewelry, etc.) into the playroom. Hang up a sheet or large scarf in a corner to create a "changing room," and place the bag of costumes inside. Explain to your child that you will use the "changing room" to hide yourselves when you are changing into a costume. Hide behind the sheet and come back out with only one thing changed. For example, you might put on a bracelet, change your socks (or simply take your socks off), or do something even subtler, like roll up your sleeves. Encourage your child to guess what is different about you. Once he has guessed correctly, switch roles and ask him go into the "changing room" to continue the game. Take turns changing and guessing until all the costumes have been used.

Variation: If your child likes competition, keep score on paper. For example, allow 1–2 chances to guess what is different about the other person and 1 point for each correct guess. The first person to get 5 points is the winner! Also, if it is difficult to hang a sheet in the playroom, simply ask your child to turn around while you change—but no peeking!

Props:
- ☐ Bag of costumes
- ☐ Sheet/large scarf

Notes:

☆147 What's Wrong Here?

Props:
- ☐ Sequencing series game
- ☐ Tape

Notes:

Challenge: Interactive attention span of 20 minutes or longer

Motivation: Pictures, hearing a story in the wrong order, putting things in order, anticipation

How to Play: Select 5–6 sequence series from any story sequencing game. Mix up the cards from the first sequence so that they are in a random order. For example, the mixed-up sequence might begin with a picture of someone eating cake. The next picture would show someone putting a cake in the oven and the last picture would show someone mixing the batter. Tape the cards in random order to a wall within your child's view. Use the cards to tell a silly story to your child. For the silly sequence given above, the story might be as follows: "One day a boy ate a cake, and then he put it in the oven and then he mixed the batter!" Ask your child to explain to you the correct order of the sequence cards. After he has explained how to rearrange the cards, retell the story in the correct order. Continue with all of the sequencing series cards.

☆148 What Goes Together?

Props:
- ☐ 5–7 card sets of associated items
- ☐ Tape
- ☐ Large poster board

Notes:

Challenge: Interactive attention span of 20 minutes or longer

Motivation: Pictures, rides, completing a chart

How to Play: Make (or buy) 5–7 picture card sets of associated items (for example, shovel/pail, raincoat/umbrella, winter hat/winter scarf). Tape some of the cards onto a wall within your child's view but out of his reach. Tape the associated item cards onto another wall within your child's view but out of his reach. Draw 5–7 rectangle outlines on a large poster board and tape it onto a third wall. Ask your child to select a card from the first wall (for example, a shovel). Have him search on the next wall for the card showing the associated item (for example, the pail). Once he has found the set, give him a piggyback ride to the matching cards, so that he can reach and pull the cards down. Give him another ride to the poster, so that he can tape the set of cards into one of the rectangle outlines. Continue until the poster has been filled with all the associated item card sets.

Variation: Before you give your child a ride to pick an associated item, ask him to explain why the items go together. For an additional challenge, use card sets that match professions with their associated tools (for example, firefighter/fire hose or doctor/stethoscope).

‹149› Cooking Class

Challenge: Interactive attention span of 20 minutes or longer

Motivation: Food!

How to Play: Write up a recipe card for a simple dish that you can make with your child. Be sure to have all the ingredients prepared and ready to be used. Assist your child in following the directions on the recipe card. For example, you might choose to make potato salad together. Work with your child to cut up the cooked potatoes, put them in a bowl and add dressing. (Other good, simple recipe choices are egg salad, fruit salad or sandwiches.) When you are done, take a picture of the finished product. Tape the recipe and the picture onto a piece of colored paper. Every time you have "cooking class," you can create similar recipe pages. Eventually, you can compile all the pages into your own recipe book!

Variation: After your child has learned a recipe, let him lead an actual cooking class. He can teach a different team member how to make the new food!

Props:
- ❏ Aprons
- ❏ Kitchen utensils as needed
- ❏ Card
- ❏ Camera

Notes:

‹150› Pack Your Bags, We're Going on a Trip!

Challenge: Interactive attention span of 20 minutes or longer

Motivation: Learning about interesting, new places, packing a bag, imaginary play

How to Play: Choose a post card/picture of an exotic place. Tell your child three facts about the new place. The facts can be about the climate, what people do there, what they grow or which language they speak. For example, show him a picture of Hawaii and tell him that Hawaii is a warm and sunny place, that people often surf in the big waves and that they grow coconut, mango and pineapple. Bring in an empty suitcase and a bag containing travel items. Include some clothing appropriate for the chosen location (for example, a bathing suit) and some inappropriate for that particular place (for example, a winter hat). Tell your child that you are going on a trip to Hawaii. Take out each item from the bag and ask your child to determine whether it is needed or not. Pack the suitcase together with your child. Then, go on a pretend plane ride to Hawaii. When you land, pretend that you are doing the activity you spoke about (surfing). Then, "fly" back and repeat the process with a different destination—like the North Pole!

Props:
- ❏ 2–3 pictures of exotic locations
- ❏ Suitcase and bag of possible travel items

Notes:

 # ☆151☆ Help a Friend

Props:
- ❏ 5–10 blank cards
- ❏ Markers
- ❏ Props as needed

Notes:

Challenge: Comforting another person when he is hurt or upset

Motivation: Role-play, interesting scenarios

How to Play: Prepare 5–10 cards with different social scenarios written on them. The scenarios should be cases in which a friend would need help or comfort. For example, you might include "One friend is playing with his favorite doll and suddenly the arm breaks off," or "A friend is eating a snack and begins to choke." Pick a card and read it to your child. Encourage your child to come up with ideas of how to help/comfort that friend. Act out the scenario using your child's ideas. Take turns role-playing the friend who needs help and the friend who offers help. Continue playing until you have acted out all the scenarios.

Creative Closet Prop List

Crafts/art supplies:

- ☐ Paper
- ☐ Pens
- ☐ Tape
- ☐ Markers
- ☐ Envelopes (5–6)
- ☐ Blank cards (40)
- ☐ Cardboard

Recommended toys/games:

- ☐ Animal picture cards
- ☐ Yoga cards
- ☐ Beach ball/basket ball
- ☐ Musical instrument
- ☐ Hula-hoop rings (3)
- ☐ Jump rope
- ☐ Puzzle (5–6 pieces)
- ☐ Doctor's kit
- ☐ Play food
- ☐ Play dishes

Other:

- ☐ Medium-sized box
- ☐ Bags (2)
- ☐ Basketball hoop/bucket
- ☐ Small cardboard box
- ☐ Large, thin blanket
- ☐ Tray
- ☐ Heavy objects (such as books or water bottles)
- ☐ Toilet paper
- ☐ Blind fold
- ☐ Pillowcases (2)
- ☐ Ping-pong balls/cotton balls (3–4)
- ☐ Table cloth
- ☐ Apron
- ☐ Dice
- ☐ Stick

Play Date Games

Guidelines for a Play Date

The games in Stages 1–4 have been geared toward helping your child become skilled and successful in fundamental social skills. Once your child has reached stage 4 in his skill level, it is time to integrate play dates into your program. The overall objective of play dates is twofold. Firstly, you want to create a safe, intimate environment, so that your child can develop a friendship with a peer more easily. Equally important, you want to help your child to take the skills that he has learned to use with adults, and transfer them into playtime with a peer. Below are basic guidelines for creating and integrating effective play dates into your child's program. Enjoy watching your child develop the skill your entire program has been striving for—making friends!

Part I: Setting up the Play Date

Where do I find the right child for a play date?

- **Family:** If there are cousins who would be appropriate, recruit them. You can also ask your family members if they know children who would be appropriate (e.g., children in their neighborhood, children of friends, etc.).

- **Neighborhood:** Seek out children in your neighborhood, especially those that your child might already have had exposure to/interest in from the neighborhood playground, etc.

- **Team members:** Ask the people on your team (workers or volunteers) if they know of children in their family or through friends. Some team members also may work at a school and have exposure to quite a few children who would be appropriate.

- **Other ideas:** Consider children from the local pool, community center, temple/church or even siblings of your other children's friends.

What type of child am I looking for?

- The ideal child for a play date is one who is within a year's age of your child and, based on what you have seen or been told, is a generally pleasant, cooperative and willing child. Children who are too controlling, aggressive or dominant will not work well, nor will children who are too shy and unwilling to participate enthusiastically in your games. The ideal child is one in whom your child has shown some interest. Go along with your child's preference if possible; if he relates to girls, try to find a girl!

Note: Some families have attempted to set up play dates with other children who also have social challenges. In our experience, this is not effective. This not only makes facilitating harder for you (since you will have two children with challenges), but it also does not provide your child with a peer who can demonstrate strong social skills.

How do I approach the parent?

- Ask your contact person (team member/family member) to initiate and explain: "I know of/am working with a family with a child who could use some help with social/friendship skills. We are looking for another child who is pleasant and cooperative, in order to invite him/her to play with this child. Would it be okay if the mother calls you to see if you would be interested?"

- If the parent agrees, call him/her and explain that you would like to set up a play date for about 45 minutes to 1 hour. Explain that you will facilitate games between the two children; so that it will be fun for his/her child and a good learning opportunity for yours. If you find that the child is a good match, try setting up a regular play date about once a week.

Note: Some parents have expressed concern about telling the other parent about their child's diagnosis because of many assumptions and stigmas that may exist. It is not necessary to share your child's diagnosis with the other parent—you can simply explain that your child has had some language/social delays and could use some help in this area.

What is the format of a play date?

- **Length:** In our experience, 45 minutes to 1 hour is the most effective length of time for an initial play date. This duration will allow your child enough time to gain from the experience and hopefully want more.

- **Location:** The playroom, as you know, is the ideal setting for your child to focus, and so, if possible, have the play date in the playroom. This also allows you the opportunity to leave the room during free play or snack time and watch how your child is interacting from your observation window. The exception would be if your playroom is too small for two children to play in freely or if your child is too inflexible in the playroom and expects to have total control there (e.g., no other child may touch his toys). If so, try having the play date in another enclosed, non-distracting room in your house when no other children are around.

- **Breaking up the time:** An effective way to utilize the time is as follows:

  9:00–9:20 (structured game facilitated by you)
  9:20–9:30 (drink/snack)
  9:30–9:45 (free play)

Note: Some parents have experienced difficulty setting up a play date for such a short amount of time (i.e., finding parents who will agree to drop off their child and then pick them up again in 45 minutes). Simply realize that this is the ideal length of time for an initial play date, and if 45 minutes with a friend can be arranged, this is most effective. One way around the problem might be asking if the parents would like to stay during the play date. Alternatively, you can offer to bring their child home when the play date is over. Keep in mind that as your child becomes more skilled at playing with a peer, the play date can be extended to a couple of hours consisting of only free play.

Part II: Facilitating the Play Date

Play dates with a peer typically have two distinct phases. Phase I is the introductory phase. In this stage, the goals are simply to make playing with a peer as attractive as possible and to focus on some basic friendship skills. Phase II is for a child who already displays consistent interest and ability in some of the basic social skills. The games in this phase, therefore, focus on more sophisticated skills, such as conversation.

Phase I

In Phase I, the goal is for your child to experience the enjoyment of playing with a peer, in a simple, facilitated, one-on-one setting.

Which skills am I trying to encourage in Phase I?

- motivation and interest in playing with a peer
- taking turns
- following games with simple rules
- celebrating a peer
- helping a peer/working together
- eye contact with a peer
- willingness to engage in physical contact
- simple communication (for example, asking and answering questions)

What is my role in the play date?

You have several roles in facilitating play dates in Phase I. First of all, you want to help bring enthusiasm and focus to the game. You do this by playing with the children initially. However it is important to note that your role is to help only when help is needed. The ultimate goal is for your child to play directly with his friend with as little intervention as possible. If your child is succeeding and they are playing nicely together, try to become "part of the background." For example, if things are going well, you can sit in the corner of the room or even leave the room and watch from outside. It is important to be willing to create this space for your child when he shows you that he is capable and ready.

Your second role will be helping your child with any challenging issues (e.g. taking turns or coping when things do not go his way). Finally, you want to celebrate all examples of effective social skills (taking turns, helping each other, eye contact and conversation). It is important to praise both children so that your child becomes aware that the skills are also being demonstrated by his peer.

What are some examples of structured games that I can facilitate to focus on these skills?

Sample Phase I games begin with game #152 on page 110.

Phase II

Phase II is for children who have demonstrated a consistent motivation to play with a peer, as well as the ability to play games with simple rules, take turns, and maintain a strong level of eye contact. The structure of the play date is the same, however the games that you facilitate will have different goals.

Which skills I am trying to encourage in Phase II?

- Conversational skills (e.g., having a reciprocal conversation with a peer: asking questions relating to something a peer said, telling stories relating to the conversation topic, responding to questions a peer asks)

- Playing more sophisticated games (e.g., board games)

What is my role in the play date?

At this stage, try to retreat from center stage, so that the two children can interact as directly as possible. Your role is to remain in the background and intervene only when necessary. This will allow your child to grow in independence, skill and confidence.

What are some examples of structured games that I can facilitate to focus on these skills?

Sample Phase II games begin with game #167 on page 116.

⭐152 Charades (with a peer)

Props:
- ❏ Box/bag
- ❏ Pictures of animals

Notes:

Challenge: Taking turns, playing games with simple rules with a peer

Motivation: Animals, anticipation, big body movements

How to Play: This game is like Charades (game #43). Have one child pick an animal card from a box/bag and act it out, while the other child guesses what he is imitating. The children can take turns acting and guessing.

Tip: Your role is to hold the box/bag to prevent either child from spilling out all the cards at one time.

⭐153 A Play of Your Own (with a peer)

Props:
- ❏ Simple story books
- ❏ Simple props for stories

Notes:

Challenge: Taking turns, playing games with simple rules with a peer

Motivation: Stories, plays, props

How to Play: This game is like A Play of Your Own (game #89). Instead of acting out the story with your child, read the story to the children and have them act it out together.

⭐154 Basketball Writing (with a peer)

Props:
- ❏ Basketball hoop (or bucket)
- ❏ Ball
- ❏ Paper
- ❏ Pens
- ❏ Tape

Notes:

Challenge: Taking turns, playing games with simple rules—with a peer

Motivation: Basketball, words, pictures

How to Play: This game is like Basketball Writing (game #96). This time let the children take turns making baskets. Once they have completed (or guessed) one word, you can start a new one—see how many words they can get!

⭐155 Roll the Cube (with a peer)

Props:
- ❏ Cardboard box
- ❏ Markers

Notes:

Challenge: Taking turns, eye contact, playing games with simple rules with a peer

Motivation: Your child's specific motivations

How to Play: This game is like Roll the Cube (game #52). This time, have the children take turns throwing the box into the air and doing the activity the box lands on.

 156 Hot Dog Roll (with a peer)

Challenge: Taking turns, physical contact, playing games with simple rules—with a peer

Motivation: Pressure or squeezes, funny imagery

How to Play: This game is like Hot Dog Roll (game #12). Once your child is rolled up, ask the other child to pretend to put condiments on him as he massages him (light "karate chops" can be mustard and massage squeezes can be ketchup). After you have rolled your child out of the blanket, let the other child become the hot dog.

Tips: If your child is hesitant to get into the blanket, model the game with the friend first. If both children are hesitant, use a stuffed animal to demonstrate the game.

Variation: For a more advanced communication challenge, have the friend ask your child to specify which condiments to use.

Props:
❑ Large, thin blanket

Notes:

157 Follow the Leader (with a peer)

Challenge: Taking turns, eye contact, playing games with simple rules with a peer

Motivation: Big body movements, costumes, slapstick

How to Play: Ask the children to stand facing each other. Explain that one child is the leader and can make all kinds of funny body movements (e.g., waving arms in the air or marching). Instruct the other child to imitate the same movements and change his movements whenever the leader does. Continue playing until each child has had several turns being the leader.

Variation: To vary the game, you can bring in costumes (two of each) for your child to imitate as well. For example, if the leader puts on a hat and jumps up and down, than the other child would imitate by putting on a hat and jumping up and down too!

Props:
None!

Notes:

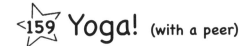 158 Heavy, Heavy, Heavy! (with a peer)

Props:
- ☐ Tray
- ☐ 4–5 heavy objects

Notes:

Challenge: Eye contact, helping each other, working together with a peer

Motivation: Carrying heavy objects

How to Play: Fill a tray with heavy objects (e.g., heavy books or big bottles of water) and place it in one corner of the room. Tell the children that you need their help bringing the water/book from one corner of the room to the other. Point out that they will need to work as a team, since it is too heavy for either one of them to carry by himself. Ask the children to each hold one end of the tray and look into each other's eyes. On the count of three, have them lift and carry the heavy tray to the other corner of the room and then unload the tray. Have them repeat the procedure until the entire load has been brought over.

Tip: Your role is to wait in the corner and pretend to drink the water or read the book once they bring the tray to you.

 159 Yoga! (with a peer)

Props:
- ☐ Yoga cards

Notes:

Challenge: Taking turns, eye contact, playing games with simple rules with a peer

Motivation: Cards, body movement

How to Play: This is like the game Yoga! (game #100). However this time, have the children take turns picking a card and then making the pose together.

Variation: Some yoga poses require two people. Bring in those cards specifically and ask the children to work together to do the poses.

160 Mummy (with a peer)

Props:
- ☐ Toilet paper

Notes:

Challenge: Taking turns, physical contact, simple communication with a peer

Motivation: Control, anticipation

How to Play: This game is like Mummy (game #45). Ask one child to stand in the middle of the room with his arms at his sides. Have the other child take the roll of toilet paper and do the mummy wrapping.

⭐161 Pin the Nose on the Face
(with a peer)

Challenge: Taking turns, playing games with simple rules with a peer

Motivation: Silliness, a favorite character

How to Play: This is like Pin the Nose on Elmo (game #98). Have the children take turns being blindfolded and attempting to pin a nose on the face of a favorite character.

Props:
- ❏ Picture of friend or character
- ❏ Paper
- ❏ Tape
- ❏ Blindfold

Notes:

⭐162 Freeze Together (with a peer)

Challenge: Taking turns, playing games with simple rules with a peer

Motivation: Big body movements, running, music

How to Play: Tell the children to run around the room and dance while you sing and play an instrument. Stop singing occasionally and instruct the children to stop and hold their position. After a few moments, begin singing again and let them resume their dancing. Let each child have a chance to be the singer/musician, while you and the other child dance.

Variation: Bring hula-hoops into the room and lay them on the floor in a path. Have the children jump from hoop to hoop while you sing, and freeze whenever you stop.

Props:
- ❏ Musical instrument

Notes:

⭐163 Relay Races (with a peer)

Challenge: Taking turns, playing games with simple rules with a peer, working together

Motivation: Doing silly activities together

How to Play: Have the children do some fun relay races together. A list of relay races can be found below.

Pillowcase Hop: Give each child a pillowcase to stand in. Send the children into opposite corners of the room. Ask them to look into each other's eyes from across the room, count to three and hop toward each other. Have them give each other a high five when they meet in the middle and then keep hopping until they reach the opposite corner. They can repeat many times by replacing the activity each time they meet in the middle (e.g., hop around each other, switch pillowcases, sing a song, etc.).

Ping-Pong Ball Pass: Give each child a plastic spoon. Direct one child to stand in one corner of the room and the other child to stand

Props:
- ❏ 2 pillowcases
- ❏ 2 spoons
- ❏ 3–4 ping-pong balls/cotton balls
- ❏ Bucket
- ❏ Light book/box

Notes:

in the middle of the room. Place a bowl or bucket at the opposite corner of the room. Give the child in the corner a ping-pong ball (or cotton ball). Have him rest the ball on the spoon and then hold the spoon carefully in his mouth. Tell him to walk to his friend without letting the ball fall off the spoon. When he reaches his friend, have him pass the ball so that the friend can continue carrying it on his own spoon. When the friend reaches the bowl/bucket at the other end of the room, he must drop it in. Repeat several times (without dropping!) until there are 3–4 balls in the bucket.

Head Balance Pass: This game is similar to Ping-Pong Ball Pass. Instead of balancing a ball on a spoon, the first child must balance something on his head (a book, box, etc.) until he reaches his friend. He then must pass it to his friend to balance until he reaches the bucket.

Wheelbarrow: Have one child balance upside down on his hands with his legs held up by his friend. Have the friend walk the human "wheelbarrow" across the room from one corner to the next.

☆164 We Are on a Mission! (with a peer)

Props:

☐ Items for your "Mission Accomplished!" party

☐ A box

Notes:

Challenge: Taking turns, playing games with simple rules, working as a team

Motivation: Having a party!

How to Play: Tell your child and his friend(s) that you will assign them five missions to find five specific items. Once all five missions are complete, you will hold a special "Mission Accomplished" party. Explain that they will each need to look for the item you specify, put it in a special box, and bring the box back to you as a team. Tell the children the first item they need to find and wait until they have brought the item to you. Then assign them the next mission. The items can be simple things, like a green leaf the size of their pinky finger, a stick the length of their hand, something purple, something soft, etc. Once the children have found all five items, celebrate with the "Mission Accomplished" party. This can be anything they will enjoy, like a special treat (popsicles) a game (water guns), etc.

⟨165⟩ Obstacle Course (with a peer)

Challenge: Taking turns, playing a game with simple rules with a peer, working together, celebrating each other

Motivation: Physical play

How to Play: Create a simple obstacle course in the room. For example, the course might consist of a table to climb under, a rope to walk along, a trampoline to jump on and a series of hula-hoops to hop across. Have the children take turns doing the course. Ask the child who is not doing the course to help his friend by cheering him on or counting for the other child to see how quickly he can complete the course.

Variation: If the children are highly motivated, they can rearrange and make new obstacle courses in order to do it again.

Props:
☐ Household objects for an obstacle course (table, chair, 3 hula-hoop rings, small slide, trampoline, rope, etc.)

Notes:

⟨166⟩ Pass the Prezzie (with a peer)

Challenge: Taking turns, playing a game with simple rules with a peer

Motivation: Getting to the present in the middle

How to Play: Choose two small, inexpensive items to be gifts for your child and his friend (such as treats, stickers, small toys, etc). Wrap the items together in one layer of wrapping paper and then write an activity on the paper (like "Sing your favorite song"). Then wrap the present in another layer of wrapping paper and write another activity on that layer. Continue this process until you have wrapped the present in 5–6 layers with activities written on each one. Explain to the children that they will sit across from each other. As and you sing a song, they pass the present back and forth to each other. When you stop singing, whoever is holding the present unwraps the first layer of paper and acts out the activity written on it. Then continue singing as the children pass the present back and forth again. When you stop singing the next time, the child holding the present unwraps the next layer and does the next activity. Play the game until the children have gotten to the presents in the middle.

Variation: This game can be played with one or more peers.

Props:
☐ 2 small presents
☐ Wrapping paper
☐ Tape
☐ Pen

Notes:

⟨167⟩ Put a Puzzle Together (with a peer)

Props:
- ☐ 5–6 envelopes
- ☐ Tape
- ☐ 5–6 puzzle pieces/ picture pieces

Notes:

Challenge: Asking/answering open-ended questions with a peer

Motivation: Puzzles, characters, animals

How to Play: This game is like Put a Puzzle Together (game #70). Have the children take turns being spun round and asking each other the questions on the cards. After they get the puzzle pieces from inside the envelope, they can assemble the puzzle together!

⟨168⟩ Doctor (with a peer)

Props:
- ☐ Doctor's kit

Notes:

Challenge: Asking/answering open-ended questions with a peer

Motivation: Doctor props

How to Play: This is like the game Doctor (game #57). Assign one child to be the doctor and the other child to be the patient. Encourage the doctor to ask the patient what is hurting and then come up with a remedy to help him. Have the children alternate roles.

⟨169⟩ Restaurant (with a peer)

Props:
- ☐ Tablecloth
- ☐ Dishes
- ☐ Pots/pans
- ☐ Play food
- ☐ Apron
- ☐ Pad of paper/pen (optional)

Notes:

Challenge: Asking/answering open-ended questions with a peer

Motivation: Imaginary play

How to Play: This game is like Restaurant (game #73). Have one child dress in an apron and be the waiter, while the other child acts as the customer. Encourage the waiter to ask the customer what he would like to eat and then serve it to him. Have the children alternate roles.

⟨170⟩ Bingo (with a peer)

Props:
- ☐ Paper
- ☐ 10 blank cards
- ☐ Small household items
- ☐ Bag

Notes:

Challenge: Playing board games with simple rules, winning/losing with a peer

Motivation: Anticipation, winning

How to Play: This game is like Bingo (game #105). Give each child a board while you take the role of "caller." Alternatively, all three of you can take turns calling numbers.

⭐171 Your Own Board Game (with a peer)

Challenge: Playing board games with simple rules, winning/losing with a peer

Motivation: Your child's favorite activities

How to Play: This is like Your Own Board Game (game #102). Let the children take turns rolling the die and moving along the board.

Props:
- ❏ Cardboard
- ❏ Markers
- ❏ Dice

Notes:

⭐172 Picture Story (with a peer)

Challenge: Cooperative story telling (working together) with a peer

Motivation: Interesting pictures, silliness, anticipation

How to Play: Prepare a box or bag of pictures (either from magazines or flashcards). Ask your child to start by picking a picture, taping it to the wall and beginning to tell a related story. Explain to him that then he will stop in the middle of his story in order to let the other child finish it for him. For example, if he picks a picture of a horse, he might say, "One day a boy rode his horse to the top of the mountain and then . . ." Ask the other child to pick the next picture, tape it to the wall, and continue the story. See what kind of silly story the children can make up together.

Tip: Your role is to hold the bag/box of pictures so that the children do not dump out all the pictures all at once. An element of anticipation will be added to the game as the children wait to see which picture is next.

Variation: At the end of the game, see if the children can tell you the whole story from the first picture to the last.

Props:
- ❏ Bag/box
- ❏ Interesting pictures
- ❏ Tape

Notes:

⭐173 Help a Friend (with a peer)

Challenge: Helping a friend, creative problem solving

Motivation: Role-play, acting

How to Play: This game is like Help a Friend (game #151). Have the children take turns being the friend who needs help and the friend who offers help. Go through all the social scenarios in this way.

Props:
- ❏ Blank cards
- ❏ Markers

Notes:

☆174 Stories in My Life (with a peer)

Props:
- ☐ 5–6 cards
- ☐ Tape

Notes:

Challenge: Telling stories relating to a conversation topic with a peer

Motivation: Hearing/sharing interesting stories, spinning

How to Play: Take six blank cards and write a conversation topic on each one. Choose topics that the children have likely experienced in their own life (for example, a visit at their grandparents' house or a time when they helped their mother, etc.). Tape the cards (face down) around the room. Ask one child to stand in the middle of the room, point his finger and stretch out his arm. Have the other child spin him gently and see which card he is pointing to (or is closest to) when he stops spinning. Read (or ask one of them to read) the topic on the card. Ask the children to take turns telling a story from their lives that relates to the topic on the card. As one child speaks, encourage the other child to listen. Have the children alternate spinning each other and selecting cards until all the conversation topics have been covered.

Tip: To help the children focus, bring them to a "conversation corner" in the room where two chairs or cushions are set up. They can use the corner for storytelling and return to the middle of the room for spinning.

☆175 Talking Stick (with a peer)

Props:
- ☐ 5–6 cards
- ☐ Stick
- ☐ Decorations

Notes:

Challenge: Telling stories relating to a conversation topic with a peer

Motivation: Holding a special stick

How to Play: Prepare a stack of cards with conversation topics written on them. Choose topics that will be familiar to the children. Decorate a special stick and designate it as a "Talking Stick." Explain to the children that you talk only if you are holding the "Talking Stick." Ask one child to hold the stick and pick a topic card. Have him tell a story relating to the topic, and pass the stick to the other child when he is done. Continue passing the stick and talking until all the conversation topics have been covered.

⟨176⟩ Show-N-Tell (with a peer)

Challenge: Asking questions relating to something a peer said, responding to questions a peer asked

Motivation: Your child's special toys

How to Play: Have each child choose 2–3 special things (toys, pictures, or articles of clothing) and put the items in a bag (you can set up the friend before the play date to bring these items from home). Put the bags on the shelf. Have each child take out one item at a time and alternate showing and discussing their special items. After each child's presentation, the other child can ask 1–2 follow-up questions to find out more about that special item.

Props:
- ❑ 2–3 special toys/pictures/articles of clothing
- ❑ 2 bags

Notes:

Frequently Asked Questions

What should I do if my child is repetitive/becomes exclusive during the play date?

If your child becomes repetitive/exclusive in the play date (for example, he starts singing "Old McDonald" over and over during a game of charades), you can:

- **Integrate your child's repetitive behavior into the game.** For example, you can say, "Old McDonald had a farm; I will act out an animal from the farm, and you guess what I am!"

- **Join in.** If your child is not interested in integrating his repetitive behavior into the game, try to see if the friend is interested in taking a break from the game. Maybe he will be willing to join in with you and your child. You can say, "Let's all sing 'Old McDonald' together, and we can play this game later." Then sing your heart out!

- **Resume the game with only the friend.** If the friend is not interested in singing your child's song and wants to continue with the game, then do not press him. You can tell your child that he can sing all he wants and that when he is finished, you would love to have him join your game again. Then simply resume the game with the other child. Every so often, invite your child to join in. This is important for several reasons. Firstly, you do not want the friend to lose interest—you want him to have fun and want to come back. Additionally, you are demonstrating to your child that he can be repetitive/exclusive if he wants AND there will be natural consequences. If he chooses to do so in the middle of a play date with a peer, the consequence will be that the game will go on without him. He is free to join in when he is ready.

What is free play?

Free play is an opportunity for your child to play with a peer without specific instructions or guidelines from you. You can ask the children (or decide yourself) which toys they would like to play with. For example, you might offer them a kitchen set, some plastic food, and maybe some dolls. Avoid offering too many choices, so that the children do not get distracted by too many toys. In addition, avoid offering toys that your child typically uses repetitively or toys that he may have a particular difficulty sharing (e.g., his favorite doll).

Where do I go from here?

Once your child has demonstrated a consistent ability to play Phase II games, challenge him further by:

- arranging longer play dates, building up to several hours consisting of free play only,
- having the play dates in more stimulating environments such as the yard or a playground,
- setting up similar play dates with *two* other children.

Creative Closet Prop List

Crafts/art supplies:

☐ Paper
☐ Markers
☐ Tape
☐ Stapler
☐ Crayons
☐ Notebooks (2)
☐ Pen
☐ Bag
☐ Blank cards
☐ Comic strips (5–7)
☐ Correction fluid
☐ Poster board (10)
☐ Colored construction paper
☐ Envelopes
☐ Magazines
☐ Scissors
☐ Stickers
☐ String
☐ Medium-sized beads
☐ Wrapping paper

Recommended toys/games:

☐ Beach ball
☐ Play-dough (see recipe below)
☐ Chutes and Ladders™ board game

Other:

☐ Photos of your child (7–10)
☐ Play cash register
☐ Play microphone
☐ Stopwatch or sand timer
☐ Beach props
☐ Camp props (tent, flash light, binoculars, etc.)
☐ Play phone
☐ Bag of simple costumes (hats, scarves, glasses)
☐ Cookie cutters (3–4)
☐ Rolling pin
☐ Plates
☐ Small cardboard boxes (3)
☐ Small table
  (continued)

Stage Five Games

Recommended play-dough recipe:

1 cup flour (can use gluten-free flour)
1 cup water
1/2 cup salt
2 tsp. cream of tartar
1 Tbs. oil

Mix the dry ingredients in a saucepan. Add the oil and water and cook for three minutes on low heat (until the mixture pulls away from the pan). Knead when cool. Add drops of food coloring if you desire and knead the color into the dough.

⭐177 Feeling Album

Challenge: Answering simple questions about his feelings and actions

Motivation: Pictures, making his own album

How to Play: Go through a family photo album and select 7–10 photos of your child. Be sure to choose photos that elicit some clear emotion. For example, you might choose a picture of your child getting a present on his birthday or a picture of your child playing with his siblings. Tape each picture to a piece of paper. Tell your child that you are gong to make a "Feeling album." Put the pictures on a shelf and choose one to show your child. After he has had a chance to look at it, ask him, "How did you feel when (you got your birthday present, you were playing with your siblings, etc.)?" Encourage him to use words that describe feelings, like "Happy," or "Excited." Write down the feeling word under each picture, until you have gone through all the photo pages. Staple the pages together and leave the cover blank. Title the book "My Feeling Album" and ask your child to decorate it. Your child can then share this album with his friends, family or team members and explain what he felt on each page.

Tip: If your child finds it challenging to express his feelings or consistently uses the same description (e.g., "Happy") for each page, create a list of varied feeling words (for example, "happy, excited, anxious, surprised, peaceful, worried, etc."). Help your child pick a word from the list to describe his feelings more specifically.

Props:
- ❏ 7–10 photos of your child
- ❏ Paper
- ❏ Markers
- ❏ Tape
- ❏ Stapler

Notes:

⭐178 Back to Back

Challenge: Speaking in complete sentences, constructing original sentences

Motivation: Being the teacher and giving you instruction

How to play: Give your child 5–10 blocks or Legos® of different shapes, colors, and sizes. Tell your child he is going to be the teacher and tell you how to build exactly what he builds, but without you watching. Sit on the floor back-to-back to with your child and ask him to build a structure out of his blocks. When he is done, ask him to explain to you exactly how to build what he has built, for example, "Put the big blue block on top of the small red block." Build your structure according to his instructions. When he is done, turn around and see how the two structures match up! You can play this game again and again, taking turns being the teacher.

Tip: You can begin with a smaller number of very distinctly different blocks and increase the challenge by adding more blocks.

Props:
- ❏ 5–10 blocks or Legos® of different shapes, colors, and sizes

Notes:

⟨179⟩ Daily Journal

Props:
- ❏ 2 notebooks
- ❏ Markers/crayons
- ❏ Pen

Notes:

Challenge: Initiating and expressing emotive information

Motivation: Making his own journal

How to Play: This game takes place over the course of several days.

Choose two notebooks that can function as journals for you and for your child. Show them to your child and explain to him that you will write in these special journals at the end of each day. Decorate the covers of your journals and write your names on them. At the end of each day, encourage your child to express an emotive statement about his experiences. For example, he might say "I had fun playing ball with Tammy" or "I was upset when I lost the game." Begin by writing and reading a sentence in your journal and then ask your child to write his sentence in his journal (or dictate it to you). Feel free to draw a picture to illustrate your sentence. Continue to fill your journal for several days or even weeks!

Tip: If your child finds it challenging to produce an emotive statement, create a list of emotions on the first page of the journal (for example, "fun, exciting, interesting, upset, frustrated, tired, etc."). Your child can refer to the list for ideas when he is writing in his journal.

⟨180⟩ Show-N-Tell

Props:
- ❏ Bag
- ❏ 5–7 special items that belong to you

Notes:

Challenge: Asking questions about what another person just said

Motivation: Seeing special items that belong to you

How to Play: This game is similar to Show-N-Tell (with a peer) (game #176). This time, fill a bag with 5–7 special things of your own. Take out one item at a time and tell your child what it is, and why it is special to you. After you have finished talking, tell your child he can ask as many questions as he would like to find out more about this special item. Continue until you have shown all of your items.

Tip: If your child does not seem to have any questions about your special item, you can prompt him by saying things like, "Someone very special gave me this gift. If you want to know who, just ask!"

☆181 Show-N-Tell II

Challenge: Answering questions

Motivation: Presenting special items that belong to him

How to Play: This game is similar to the Show-N-Tell described above, but this time your child will be able to present his special items.

Give your child a bag and explain to him that he will be filling it with 5–7 special items. Ask him to go around the house or the playroom and collect things that he wants to show you (toys, books, dolls, etc.). Put your child's bag on the shelf. Bring down the bag before each round so he can select one item at a time. Ask him to take out the first item. Encourage him to tell you what it is, and why it is special to him. After your child has finished presenting, ask him several questions to find out more about this special item. Continue until your child has shown and presented all of his items.

Props:
❑ Bag
❑ 5–7 special items that belong to your child

Notes:

☆182 A Zoo of My Own

Challenge: Answering questions

Motivation: Your child's favorite animals, teaching others

How to Play: Print out five pictures of your child's favorite animals. Alternatively, you can collect five favorite stuffed animals. Make an information card for each animal containing several interesting facts (e.g., where they come from, what they eat, etc.). Help your child create his "zoo" by setting up the pictures (or arranging the animals) all over the room and taping each information card next to the corresponding animal. Tell your child that you are a visitor at the zoo and that he is the zookeeper. His job will be to give you a tour of the zoo's animals and tell you all the information he knows about each animal. Go out of the room and come back in as a zoo visitor. Ask your child to give you a tour of the zoo's animals. After your child has finished presenting each animal, ask him several questions to find out more information. For example, you might ask him "What is this animal's name?" or "How long has this elephant been at your zoo?" Continue playing until your child has presented each animal and has answered all of your questions.

Props:
❑ 5 animal pictures
❑ 5 cards
❑ Tape
❑ Table
❑ Zookeeper hat (optional)

Notes:

Variation: If your child is especially motivated by imaginary play, give him a zookeeper hat to wear. You can also set up a "ticket booth" for him to operate. Make sure to pay for your ticket before entering the zoo!

⟨183⟩ A Zoo of My Own II

Props:
☐ 5 animal pictures
☐ 5 cards
☐ Tape
☐ Table
☐ Zookeeper hat (optional)

Notes:

Challenge: Asking questions about what another person just said

Motivation: Your child's favorite animals

How to Play: This game is like the one above—but this time you are the zookeeper.

Print out five pictures of your child's favorite animals. Alternatively, you can collect five favorite stuffed animals. Make an information card for each animal containing several interesting facts (e.g., where they come from, what they eat, etc.). Create a "zoo" by setting up the pictures (or arranging the animals) all over the room and taping each information card next to the corresponding animal. Tell your child that you are the zookeeper at the zoo and that he is the visitor. Your job will be to give him a tour of the zoo's animals and tell him all the information you know about each animal. After you have finished presenting each animal, encourage your child to ask several questions to find out more information. Continue playing until you have presented each animal in this way.

Tip: If your child has a hard time coming up with questions, you can give one or two pieces of information from your fact card, like the life span of this particular animal and leave out the other information so your child can ask about those pieces.

⟨184⟩ A Museum of My Own

Props:
☐ 5 dinosaur pictures
☐ 5 cards
☐ Tape
☐ Table
☐ Play microphone

Notes:

Challenge: Answering questions

Motivation: Dinosaurs, teaching others

How to Play: This is game is similar to A Zoo of My Own above, but this time you will be creating a dinosaur museum instead of a zoo.

Print out five dinosaur pictures. Make an information card for each dinosaur containing several interesting facts about each one (e.g., what they are called, what they eat, their typical life span, etc.). Help your child create a "museum" by setting up the pictures all over the room and taping each fact sheet next to the corresponding dinosaur. Tell your child that you are a visitor at the museum and he is the tour guide. Go out of the room and come back in as a visitor. Ask your child to give you a tour of the museum's dinosaurs. After your child has finished presenting each dinosaur, ask him several questions to find out more. Continue playing until your child has presented each dinosaur and answered all of your questions.

Variation: If your child is especially motivated by imaginary play, you can give your child a play microphone to use during his tour. You can also set up a "ticket booth" for him to operate.

<185 A Museum of My Own II

Challenge: Asking questions about what another person just said

Motivation: Dinosaurs

How to Play: This game is like the one above, but this time you are the tour guide.

Print out pictures of five of dinosaurs and set up a museum as above. After you have given your presentation on each dinosaur, ask your child what he would like to ask to find out more. Continue until you have given your presentation on each dinosaur and your child has asked you questions abut each one.

Tip: If your child has a hard time coming up with questions, you can give one or two pieces of information from your fact card, like how long this dinosaur usually lives for' and leave out the other information so your child can ask about those pieces.

Props:
- ❏ 5 dinosaur pictures
- ❏ 5 cards
- ❏ Tape
- ❏ Table
- ❏ Play microphone

Notes:

<186 Your Very Own Comic Strip

Challenge: Making statements that are clearly relevant to the conversation topic

Motivation: Cartoons

How to Play: Collect several newspaper comic strips that you think your child would enjoy. Cut them out and use correction fluid to erase all the words that are written in the bubbles (you can make the comics more legible by photocopying and enlarging them). Put the prepared comic strips (with empty bubbles) onto the shelf. Show your child the first comic strip and explain to him that you will need to work together to imagine the conversations that were erased from the bubbles. Bring down one at a time and take turns filling out the bubbles to make a conversation that is related to the pictures. Make sure that the dialogue ideas that your child presents are clearly related to the comic strip pictures. Continue until you and your child have filled in the bubbles on all the comic strips. When you have finished, staple the pages together to make your very own comic book.

Variation: You can make your own comic strip! Pick a topic that your child is familiar with (e.g., a slumber party or a visit to the pet store) and draw 4–5 empty frames. Sketch pictures of possible characters that correspond with the story and add empty bubbles for the dialogue. Fill in the bubbles together with your child.

Tip: To help your child understand how comics work, first bring in several intact comic strips. Explain that the bubbles represent conversation. You can read the bubbles that belong to one character, and let your child read the others. Acting out the comic strip in this way can help your child visualize the scenes better.

Props:
- ❏ 5–7 comic strips
- ❏ Correction fluid
- ❏ Pen
- ❏ Paper

Notes:

 Hot Debate

Props:

☐ 5–10 cards
☐ Pen
☐ Small table

Notes:

Challenge: Expressing opinions within a conversation

Motivation: Hearing your opinion, winning

How to Play: Bring in 5–10 cards with a debate topic written on each one and put them on a "podium" (a small table). Pick debate topics that will interest your child, such as "What is the most fun game to play, and why?" or "What is your favorite season—summer or winter, and why?"). Pick a debate card, stand at the podium and communicate your opinion on that topic. Then, give your child the same card and have him express his own opinion on the matter. Continue until you have gone through all the debate topic cards.

Variation: If your child likes competition, invite a third person to hear the debates. After you have both presented each topic, he can award points to the most convincing speaker. Keep score and see who has the most points at the end of the debate tournament.

Problem Solving Agency

Props:

☐ Small table
☐ Two chairs
☐ Play phone
☐ Paper
☐ Pen
☐ Simple costumes (hats/scarves/glasses)

Notes:

Challenge: Expressing opinions within a conversation

Motivation: Hearing funny problems, being the "expert"

How to Play: Set up a table and two facing chairs. Make the table into an office by placing "office" items on it (e.g., a play phone, paper, pen, etc.). Make a hat or sign for the table that says "Problem Solving Expert." Tell your child that he will be the "Problem Solving Expert" and that he will be responsible for giving wise advice to people with problems. Explain that the advice he gives will be his opinion and that there is no right or wrong answers. Leave the room, put on a funny costume and come back in dressed as a character with an interesting problem. Be creative—remember, you are trying to spark your child's imagination. Your problem might be that you cannot fall asleep because the neighbor's dog starts to bark every time you get into bed, or you are having a hard time hearing because you get water in your ears whenever you take a bath. Ask your child for his expert opinion on how to solve your problem. Thank him enthusiastically for his advice, leave the room and return as a different character with a new problem. After several rounds, switch roles and then you can be the "Problem Solving Expert!"

⭐189 Name That Tone

Challenge: Speaking using varying intonations (not monotone)

Motivation: Silly sentences, guessing, winning

How to Play: Prepare a stack of 10 cards with a silly sentence written on each one (for example, "Frog soup is yummy," or "The dog is wearing pink slippers"). Prepare another stack of 4–5 cards with a feeling written on each one (for example, "Excited," "Sad," "Afraid" or "Bored"). Put the "Sentence" cards into one bag/box and the "Feeling" cards into another bag/box. Pick a "Sentence" card and read it to your child. Then pick a "Feeling" card without showing or telling him what it says. Reread your original sentence using the emotions written on the "Feeling" card that you picked. Ask your child to guess what the feeling was, based on the intonation in your voice. Take turns picking and reading until all the sentence cards have been used.

Variation: If your child likes competition, you can keep score. Points can be earned for every correct guess. The player with the most points is the winner!

Props:
❑ 15 cards
❑ Two bags/boxes
❑ Paper
❑ Pen

Notes:

⭐190 Where Are We Now?

Challenge: Initiating conversation appropriate to the social context

Motivation: Your child's favorite imaginary play, slapstick

How to Play: Make 3–4 signs that represent different social settings. For example, the signs might read "Dr. Rosen's Doctor Office," "Sillyville Movie Theatre!" or "Welcome to the Community Pool." Choose two props that match each social context (for example, two sick baby dolls/doctor's office, two tickets/movie theater or two towels/pool). Put all the props into a bag and place it on a shelf. Tape the first sign to the wall, and give one corresponding prop to your child and one to yourself. Explain to your child that the sign indicates where he will be "going" today. Tell him that the "trip" will begin as soon as he starts the conversation. Hold your prop in an interesting way (for example, put the towel on your head or hold the movie tickets with a very excited expression on your face) and then freeze and wait. Let your child initiate the conversation. He might ask something like "Which movie are we going to see?" Once he has, begin acting out an imaginary scene in that social setting. Make it as silly/interesting as possible (for example, do triple flips into the swimming pool or spill popcorn all over yourself at the movie). Continue dramatizing the scene until it reaches a natural end (for example, both of your babies get checked by the doctor or you both finish swimming in the pool). Then put up a new sign, hand out new props and "enter" a new social setting. Continue until you have acted out all the scenes together.

Props:
❑ 3–4 pieces of poster board
❑ 2 props corresponding to each scene

Notes:

⟨191⟩ Three-Way Conversation Pass

Props:
- ❏ 5–10 cards
- ❏ Pen
- ❏ Beach ball

Notes:

Challenge: Being able to follow and contribute to a three-way conversation

Motivation: Playing ball, trying to get you to drop the ball

How to Play: This game is to be played by three people. Prepare a stack of cards with different conversation topics written on each one. Choose topics that your child is familiar with, such as a family trip, fun things to do at the beach, and a time when you were sick. Have all the players stand in a triangular formation and place a beach ball on the floor in the center. Explain to your child that the player holding the beach ball is the one who speaks—everyone else listens. Each person will have a turn picking a new conversation card (starting with you and going around counter clockwise) after each round. Begin by picking a conversation card, holding the beach ball and talking about the topic while the other two players listen (for up to 1 minute). Then, throw the ball to the next player. When he catches it, he can begin talking about the same topic until he throws the ball to the third player. The third player continues to add to the same conversation topic. Then, and here is the twist, the ball is passed back to you. The child who will pick the next conversation card must first get the ball from you. Hold the ball tightly between your knees and ask him to tickle you or knock the ball out, until you drop it. Once he has, he picks a new topic card and the next round begins. Continue until you have gone through all the conversation cards.

⟨192⟩ Stand Up Comedy

Props:
- ❏ Poster board
- ❏ 9 printed jokes
- ❏ Tape
- ❏ Markers

Notes:

Challenge: Understanding humor

Motivation: Hearing funny jokes, choosing categories

How to Play: Find nine kids' jokes and print them out (from the Internet or from a joke book). Make sure to choose jokes that can be categorized into three different categories (for example, 3 animal jokes, 3 food jokes and 3 knock-knock jokes). Draw three columns on a poster board and label them accordingly (for example, "Animal Jokes," "Food Jokes" and "Knock-knock Jokes"). Tape each joke (face down) onto its poster column and tape the poster board to the wall. Ask your child to look at the poster and pick a joke category. Read him one of the jokes from that category and explain it to him if necessary (i.e., if he does not understand what makes it funny). You may need to explain humor techniques such as "a play on words." Continue until you have told your child all the jokes. At the end, have your child vote and choose the funniest joke.

⟨193⟩ Stand Up Comedy II

Challenge: Understanding humor

Motivation: Performing for the family

How to Play: The day before you play this game, have your child choose three joke categories (for example, animal jokes, food jokes and knock-knock jokes). Use the Internet or a joke book to choose nine jokes (3 from each category). Draw three columns on a poster board and label them accordingly (for example, "Animal Jokes," "Food Jokes" and "Knock-knock Jokes"). Tape each joke (face down) onto its poster column. Pick a date and time for your child's comedy show. Set up chairs for the audience (the family) and have your child do his own stand up routine. Let the audience pick the categories and your child read the appropriate jokes. Make sure to applaud his show when he is done!

Tip: Have a dress rehearsal with your child before the show so that he is familiar with the jokes and feels prepared. If your child does not read, act as the comedy assistant and whisper the joke into his ear each time a category is selected. Then, stand to the side while he repeats it in a loud voice to the audience. You can also make his show into a real performance by issuing tickets and providing popcorn!

Props:
- ❑ 15 cards
- ❑ 2 bags/boxes
- ❑ Paper
- ❑ Pen

Notes:

⟨194⟩ Calendar of Friends

Challenge: Expressing appreciation to others

Motivation: Having and using his very own calendar

How to Play: This is more of a project idea than a game, as it can be done over the course of a year. Search for a computer program to create personalized calendars. Make a calendar for your child so that each month has a picture of your child and one of his friends or family members. Create a list of birthdates of your children's friends, team members, and family. Enter the dates into his personalized calendar. Give your child this calendar as a present and tell him that each day you will check it together to see if it is someone's birthday. If it is, you can come up with an idea together of how you would like to honor that person; you can make a card together, create a present, or call the friend and sing "Happy Birthday!"

This project was inspired by a family calendar I made for my grandmother's 88th birthday. She loved this personalized gift. It is a great way to help your child consider the people in his life and express his love and gratitude to them.

Props:
- ❑ A calendar made from an on-line program

Notes:

⭐195 Thank You Cards

Props:
- ❑ Several pieces of colored construction paper
- ❑ Markers
- ❑ Stickers

Notes:

Challenge: Expressing appreciation to others

Motivation: Drawing, stickers, art

How to Play: Set up a table with several sheets of colored construction paper, markers and stickers. In order to model to your child what it is you want him to do, think of someone you want to express gratitude to and write the thank you message on the card. Then, ask your child to think of someone in his life to whom he would like to express gratitude to. The reason for gratitude can be very simple, such as Grandma always making his favorite cookies. Assist your child in writing the thank you message on the card and let him decorate it. Your child can either give the card to his friend/family member when he sees them next, or you can mail it to them. Continue to make several cards this way.

Tip: If your child has a hard time thinking of someone to thank, you can help him choose from a list of names or a series of pictures of friends/family members. Make sure to use crafts that your child enjoys working with, but avoid anything too messy or anything that encourages exclusive play.

⭐196 Appreciation Presents

Props:
- ❑ Several copies of your child's picture
- ❑ Several pieces of colored construction paper/cardboard
- ❑ Tape/glue
- ❑ Crafts (markers, stickers, etc.)

Notes:

Challenge: Expressing appreciation to others

Motivation: Drawing, stickers, art

How to Play: Print out several copies of your child's picture, with enough room on the rest of the paper to write a message. Cut out several rectangular "picture frames" to fit the picture pages using cardboard or construction paper. Place the frames and pictures onto a shelf in the room. Begin by telling your child to whom you would like to give an appreciation present and what you want to thank them for. Then, ask your child to think of someone in his life to whom he would like to give an appreciation present. Once your child has chosen the person, ask him what he would like to thank them for. Assist your child in writing his thoughts on the picture page. Then, let your child pick a frame and decorate it with crafts (for example, stickers or markers). Tape/glue the personalized frame onto the picture page and have your child give it to the recipient when he sees him next. Continue to make several presents this way.

Tip: If your child has a hard time thinking of someone to thank, you can help him choose from a list of names or a series of pictures of friends/family members. Make sure to use crafts that your child enjoys, but avoid anything too messy or anything that encourages exclusive play.

⟨197⟩ Appreciation Board

Challenge: Expressing appreciation to others

Motivation: Making and receiving mail

How to Play: Take a large poster board and hang it in your child's room. Write "Appreciation Board" on the top, and glue several envelopes or pockets to it. Label the different envelopes/pockets with the names of your team members/family. At the end of each day, write an appreciation note to a specific person, read it aloud to your child and put the note into his pocket/envelope. Then, ask your child to do the same. When team/family members come to play with your child, they can check the board and see if there is a note for them. If there is, encourage them to read it out loud and enjoy the note together with your child.

Variation: Add an envelope/pocket with your child's name on it so that your team members/family members can write notes to your child. Feel free to write your child/team members some appreciation notes as well!

Props:
- ❏ Large poster board
- ❏ Envelopes (enough for everyone on your team and family)
- ❏ Markers
- ❏ Glue/tape

Notes:

Interactive Attention Span

⟨198⟩ Things I Like

Challenge: Having a "typical" duration of interaction or higher within a single activity chosen by another person

Motivation: Choosing interesting pictures

How to Play: Take two poster boards and hang them in your child's room. Write your name on top of one of the posters and your child's name on the other. Bring in an assortment of magazine pictures. Begin the game by picking a picture that you like. Then, cut it out, explain to your child what you like about the picture and then tape it to your poster. Then, have your child do the same. Continue until you have both filled your posters.

Variation: In order to help your child consider another perspective, you can play a version of this game called The Things That You Might Like. Take turns picking out pictures that you think the other player might like, explain why you think so and tape it to their board.

Tip: If your child tends to get repetitive with letters/words, try selecting pictures from magazines without much text—or simply print pictures from the Internet.

Props:
- ❏ 2 large poster boards
- ❏ Tape
- ❏ Magazines
- ❏ Scissors

Notes:

⭐199 My Very Own Bakery

Props:
- ❏ Play-dough (see recipe in creative closet prop list)
- ❏ 3 cookie cutters
- ❏ Rolling pin
- ❏ Small boxes
- ❏ 3 plates
- ❏ Poster board
- ❏ Markers
- ❏ Tape
- ❏ Play cash register

Notes:

Challenge: Having a "typical" duration of interaction or higher within a single activity chosen by another person

Motivation: Using play-dough, imaginary play

How to Play: Place a play cash register on the table and stack some empty small boxes on the side. Set up some play-dough (either store-bought or home-made), a rolling pin, three different cookie cutters and three plates. Tell your child that he will be setting up his own bakery—but first you will help him make the cookies. Work with your child to roll out the dough and cut "cookies" using the different cookie cutters. Fill each plate with a different type of cookie (for example, star, heart and diamond cookies). Tell your child that you are a customer and ask him which cookies he has for sale. Order the cookies that you would like and have your child pack them in a box for you. Your child can use the play cash register to tell you how much the cookies cost—pay for your cookies and gobble them up! When your child is done, switch roles and let him be the customer.

Variations: To extend the bakery game even further, help your child make a sign to hang in the bakery shop, or come up with different cookie designs (e.g., crisscross them with a fork or use dots as sprinkles).

Tip: If your child tends to play repetitively with play-dough, make cookies out of cardboard instead. You can use different shaped stencils to make the different cookie types.

⭐200 My Very Own Jewelry Shop

Props:
- ❏ String
- ❏ Beads
- ❏ Scissors
- ❏ Poster board
- ❏ Tape
- ❏ Play cash register
- ❏ Play money
- ❏ Wrapping paper/ bags (optional)

Notes:

Challenge: Having a "typical" duration of interaction or higher within a single activity chosen by another person

Motivation: Making jewelry, imaginary play

How to Play: Collect an assortment of materials for making jewelry (e.g., string, assorted beads, etc.). Work with your child to make a variety of necklaces and bracelets and pack them each into a separate box. Make a sign for your jewelry store and tell your child that you are a costumer. Ask your child to show you the jewelry he has for sale and select a piece of jewelry. Your child can use the play cash register to tell you how much it will cost. Pay for your jewelry and then switch roles.

Tip: If your child tends to play repetitively with beads, put the beads on the shelf and only give him 7–10 beads at a time (he can request them by color).

Mad Libs

Challenge: Having a "typical" duration of interaction or higher within a single activity chosen by another person

Motivation: Making up silly stories

How to Play: Write out several one-page stories and leave blank spaces for your child to fill in the missing words. A sample story can be found below.

> One day, (name of friend) went to the pet shop to buy a (type of animal). She looked all over the pet shop but could not find what she wanted; all they seemed to have were (type of animal). She asked the pet shop owner where she could find what she was looking for, and he said that all they had today were (color) dogs, (color) cats and (color) birds. She decided to buy a (color) (type of animal). She loved her new pet and fed it (type of food) everyday as she was told.

Ask your child to give you each missing piece of information and write it down on the corresponding blank. When you are done, read the resulting story to your child. Continue until you have filled in and read all the stories.

Variation: If your child is familiar with grammar (e.g., nouns, verbs and adjectives), you can ask him to provide that specific piece of information (for example, "One day, [noun] went to the pet shop . . .").

Props:
❑ Paper
❑ Pen

Notes:

Pictionary

Challenge: Having a "typical" duration of interaction or higher within a single activity chosen by another person

Motivation: Anticipation/guessing, drawing, winning

How to Play: Think of 7–10 words that can be accompanied by concrete drawings (for example, "birthday cake" or "bathtub"). Write the words onto 7–10 cards and put the cards into a bag or box. Set up approximately 10 sheets of paper on the table. Pick a card out of the bag/box and read the word—but do not tell your child what the word is. Begin drawing the picture while your child tries to guess what it is. Continue until he has guessed the word correctly and then switch. Keep playing until you have gone through all the cards.

Variation: You can add some excitement to the game by making it timed. Use a stopwatch (or a sand timer) to give your child 1 minute to guess what the drawing is. In order to earn a point, he must guess it correctly before the time is up. Keep track of the points—the player with the most points is the winner! If you want to make the game more challenging, do not allow the drawer to help the guesser with any verbal clues. Lastly, for children who do not yet read, draw pictures on the cards instead of writing words.

Tip: Try using words that your child finds particularly motivating.

Props:
❑ Box/bag
❑ 7–10 cards
❑ 10 pieces of paper
❑ Pen/pencil
❑ Stopwatch/sand timer (optional)

Notes:

 Trivia Game Show

Props:
- [ ] Poster board
- [ ] Tape
- [ ] 10–15 cards
- [ ] Pen/pencil

Notes:

Challenge: Having a "typical" duration of interaction or higher within a single activity chosen by another person

Motivation: Topics your child enjoys

How to Play: Choose three areas/topics that your child enjoys (e.g., cars, spelling and math) and use them to make your own game show trivia board. Divide a poster board into three columns and label the columns with the topics that you have selected. Create three question cards for each topic, making sure that the questions have varying levels of difficulty. Include one easy question (for 1 point) one medium question (for 2 points) and one challenging question (for 3 points). Indicate the number of points the question is worth by writing it on the back of the question card. A sample set of leveled questions can be found below:

> Spelling column
>
> How do you spell "cat?" (1 point)
>
> How do you spell "bike?" (2 points)
>
> How do you spell "house?" (3 points)

Tape the cards face down (with only their numbers visible) in the corresponding columns. Tape the board to the wall and tell your child that you will be hosting a trivia game show and that he will be a contestant. Ask your child to pick a category and a point level in order to start the game (for example, "Spelling for 3 points"). Read your child the question and give him the points if he gets the answer correct. Continue until you have gone through all the cards on your board and see how many points he can earn!

Variation: You can expand your board (for example, create 4–5 levels of difficulty or add another category) and/or play with two contestants, such as your child and another team member. Score the points at the end and see who wins! If your child can read, create the board and have him host the game show—while you and/or a family member play as contestants.

Flexibility

⟨204⟩ Chutes and Ladders

Challenge: Being flexible within another's activity

Motivation: Anticipation, winning

How to Play: Either buy a Chutes and Ladders™ game board or make your own. To make your own, take a large poster board and make a snake path with approximately 30 spaces between the start and finish. Along the path, draw a ladder that will carry a player ahead and also make slides ("chutes") which, if landed on, will make a player go several spaces back. Take turns rolling a die and moving as many spaces as the die indicates—if you land on a ladder, move ahead, and if you land on a chute, slide down. Play until the first person reaches the finish!

Props:
- ☐ Chutes and Ladders™ game board (or poster board, die and 2 pawns)

Notes:

⟨205⟩ Freeze and Switch!

Challenge: Being flexible within another's activity (easily allows peripheral variations within another's activity)

Motivation: Art projects, anticipation

How to Play: Tape a large and wide piece of paper to the lower part of the wall (so that it is easily reachable if you are sitting on the floor). Collect 3–4 cards and label each card with the name of a different art supply (e.g., "crayons," "markers," "stickers" or "stencils"). Collect all of the art supplies listed on the cards and put them onto a shelf in the room along with the envelope. Tell your child you are going to draw a beautiful mural together—but there is a twist! Explain to him that this is a "freeze and switch" mural. You will begin working, and then you will have to "freeze" (stop what you are doing) and "switch" (begin using a different art supply). Set a timer for 4–5 minutes and pick the first card from the envelope. Begin working on the mural with the supply that was indicated on the card. When the timer beeps, freeze (stop using the art supply), go to the envelope, pull out a card and switch to the art supply that is written on the card (for example, switch from crayons to stickers). Then, set the timer again and continue the mural using the new art supply. Continue this process until you have used all the art supplies listed in the envelope.

Variation: If your child finds it too challenging to work on a mural together, give him his own mural to work on independently.

Props:
- ☐ 1–2 big pieces of paper
- ☐ Tape
- ☐ Envelope
- ☐ 4–5 cards
- ☐ 4–5 different art supplies
- ☐ Timer/stopwatch

Notes:

⟨206⟩ Freeze and Switch! II

Props:
- ❏ 3–4 of your child's favorite games
- ❏ Stopwatch/timer

Notes:

Challenge: Being flexible within another's activity (easily allows central variations within another's activity).

Motivation: A variety of your child's favorite games, anticipation

How to Play: This game is similar to the one above—however, this one focuses on changing a central part of the game.

Set up 3–4 play stations in the corners of the room (for example, a puzzle corner, a Lego™/blocks corner and a dolls corner). Tell your child that you will be playing a "freeze and switch" game, in which you will begin playing, and then you will have to "freeze" (stop what you are doing) and "switch" (begin playing with something else). Set a timer for 4–5 minutes and begin playing together in the first station. When the timer beeps, freeze and switch to the next station. Then, set the timer again and play in the next station until the timer beeps. Continue until have you gone to each play station at least once (you can even continue and do two rounds!).

Tip: Avoid using games that your child may play with in a repetitive way—since it may be too challenging for him to switch when the timer beeps.

⟨207⟩ Stranded on a Desert Island

Props:
- ❏ 1–2 blankets
- ❏ Various "island" props

Notes:

Challenge: Being spontaneous within another's activity, at least once per activity (initiates new ideas / direction)

Motivation: Interesting props, imaginary play

How to Play: Make a "desert island" in the room by spreading a blanket on the floor and designating everything around the blanket as "water" (you can make the "water" more realistic by using blue blankets or scarves). Fill a bag with props that you might need on your island (e.g., a pot, spoon, fork, bowl, blanket and play hammer). Explain to your child you are going to pretend that you have both been stranded on a desert island. You will have to work together to figure out how to make shelter and get food/water. Think of a creative way to find food (for example, use the bowl to try to catch "fish") and then ask your child to contribute an idea of his own. Work together in this way to think of ways to find food, make shelter or even get rescued. After each idea is proposed and agreed upon, act it out (like pretend to make a fire and cook a fish on it).

Tip: You can add props that will make it easier for your child to visualize the plans (for example, use sticks for fire or paper fish for fishing).

⭐ 208 A Day at the Beach

Challenge: Being spontaneous within another's activity, at least once per activity (initiates new ideas / direction)

Motivation: Interesting props, imaginary play

How to Play: Lay two beach towels on the floor and tell your child that you are going to have a pretend day at the beach. You can make the "beach" more realistic by taping a picture of waves, shells and sun on the walls and/or putting bathing suits on top of your clothes! Fill a beach bag with beach items (e.g., shovel and pail, an empty bottle for "sunscreen," a beach ball, a kite, or picnic materials). Suggest an activity that you can do together on the beach (for example, say "Hey, let's play with the beach ball!") and then engage your child in that activity. When you are done playing, ask your child to suggest the next activity. Continue taking turns contributing ideas and determining the direction of the game.

Tip: The activities that you suggest can be related to the props in your bag, or they can stem from your imagination. For example, you might suggest, "I will go buy us some ice cream," and come back with two imaginary cones and lick away!

Props:
- ☐ 2 beach towels
- ☐ Bag
- ☐ Beach props (such as beach ball, empty bottle for sunscreen, bathing suits, a kite, shovel and pail)
- ☐ Markers
- ☐ Paper

Notes:

⭐ 209 Let's Go Camping!

Challenge: Being spontaneous within another's activity, at least once per activity (initiates new ideas / direction)

Motivation: Interesting props, imaginary play

How to Play: Set up a tent in the room and tell your child that you are going to go on a pretend camping trip. If your playroom is big enough, put up a real tent—if not, make one using sheets and chairs. Fill a bag with camping props (e.g., flashlights, small pots, pretend bug spray, blankets/sleeping bags, sticks for a fire and cotton balls "marshmallows"). After you have set up your camping site, take turns contributing ideas for camping trip activities. The suggestions can be related to the props in your bag, or they can stem from your imagination (for example, telling spooky stories, making a fire and roasting marshmallows, looking at the stars, etc.). After each idea is proposed and agreed upon, act it out (like setting up the fire and putting marshmallows on a stick).

Props:
- ☐ Tent (or sheets/chairs to make your own)
- ☐ Camping props (such as a flashlight, sticks for a fire, a small pot, pretend marshmallows, binoculars, pretend bug spray, etc.)

Notes:

Part Three
Targeted Games

Introduction

In our years of experience working with children diagnosed on the autism spectrum or with other developmental delays, we have found that motor skills often present a challenge. Difficulties with gross and fine motor skills make daily activities, such as getting dressed or climbing stairs, much more difficult. Therefore, we have designed games to focus on these specific skills so your child will be able to grow and succeed in all areas of physical and social development!

Creative Closet Prop List

Crafts/art supplies:

☐ Tape
☐ Blank cards

Recommended toys/games:

☐ Bottle of bubbles
☐ Yoga cards
☐ 3–4 hula-hoop rings
☐ Small slide
☐ Trampoline
☐ Beach ball

Other:

☐ Jump rope (extra long)
☐ Beanbags (you can make your own by filling an old sock with un-cooked beans and tying the ends into a knot)

Gross Motor Games

⟨210⟩ Bubble Clap

Props:
❏ Bubbles

Notes:

Challenge: Clapping using both hands

Motivation: Popping bubbles

How to Play: Bring in a bottle of bubbles and tell your child that you are going to blow some bubbles and that he gets to pop them. However, these bubbles need to be popped in a special way—by clapping them! Each time that your child has clapped 10 bubbles, switch roles—he can blow bubbles and you can clap them. Ask him to count while you clap away!

⟨211⟩ Tug of War

Props:
❏ Rope
❏ Tape

Notes:

Challenge: Pulling heavy weight

Motivation: Winning!

How to Play: Bring a jump rope into the room. Put a piece of tape on the floor to mark the midline for the rope. Hold one end of the rope and ask your child to hold the other. On the count of 3, both of you begin pulling! The first person to pull the other past the tape midline is the winner!

Tip: You can extend this game by trying to use your weight in a way that allows your child to pull for a while before either of you wins.

⟨212⟩ The Snake Chase

Props:
❏ Rope

Notes:

Challenge: Jumping with two feet

Motivation: Chasing, anticipation

How to Play: Bring a jump rope into the room. Tell your child that your rope is a snake (you can even draw a snake face on the tip). Explain that this snake mostly sleeps, but that it may suddenly spring to life and catch him by his feet. Lay the rope flat on the floor and make snoring sounds. Then, start wiggling the "snake" quickly as you move after your child. Tell your child that he needs to jump with both feet to make sure that the snake does not get him!

⭐ 213 The Balloon Hop

Challenge: Jumping with two feet

Motivation: Balloons

How to Play: Demonstrate to your child how to play this game by doing it first. Bring in a balloon and throw it up in the air. Hit the balloon with your head by jumping up with two feet. See how many times you can hit the balloon with your head before the balloon falls to the ground. Then give the balloon to your child and ask him to throw the balloon in the air and try to hit it with his head by jumping with two feet. Count how many times he can hit the balloon with is head before the balloon drops to the floor. Play this game again until you can each reach a top score as high as 3, 4, or 5!

Props:
- ☐ A balloon

Notes:

⭐ 214 Land/Sea

Challenge: Jumping with two feet

Motivation: Tickles, chasing

How to Play: Use a hula-hoop to make a big circle on the floor. Tell your child that the inside of the circle is the sea and the outside of the circle is the land. In order to help your child remember this, draw pictures of fish to tape inside the circle and trees to tape outside the circle. Explain that whenever you say "Sea," he has to jump with both feet into the circle. Whenever you say "Land," he must jump with both feet outside of the circle. If he gets confused and jumps in the "Land" when you said "Sea," or vice versa, then become a big fish, chase after him and tickle him until he returns.

Props:
- ☐ Hula-hoop
- ☐ Pictures of fish
- ☐ Pictures of trees
- ☐ Tape

Notes:

⭐ 215 The Yoga Spin

Challenge: Body awareness, gross motor coordination, balance

Motivation: Anticipation, spinning

How to Play: Place 6–10 yoga cards on the floor in a big circle. Ask your child to stand in the middle of the circle, point out his finger and close his eyes (if he would like). Have him spin while you count to 3. When you are done, have him open his eyes and see which yoga card he is pointing to (or is closest to). Do the indicated yoga position together and then remove it from the circle. Continue spinning and picking until there are no more cards left in the circle.

Props:
- ☐ 6–10 yoga cards

Notes:

☆216 The Yoga Play

Props:
☐ 6–10 yoga cards depicting animals

Notes:

Challenge: Body awareness, gross motor coordination, balance

Motivation: Portraying different animals

How to Play: Pick 5–6 yoga cards that portray animal positions (i.e. "the butterfly," "the turtle," "the cat," etc.). Make up a simple story using these characters and tell it your child. As you introduce each animal in your story, show the appropriate yoga card and encourage your child to do that yoga pose. A sample story can be found below.

> One day, a frog took a walk in the woods (show the frog card and have him do the frog pose). The frog was leaping along, when all of a sudden, he felt a butterfly tickling his back (show your child the butterfly card and have him do the butterfly pose) . . .

☆217 Obstacle Course

Props:
☐ Household objects for an obstacle course (table, chair, 3 hula-hoop rings, small slide, trampoline, rope, etc.)

Notes:

Challenge: Climbing, crawling and jumping

Motivation: Cheering each other

How to Play: This game is like Obstacle Course (with a peer) (game #165). This time the two of you can take turns completing the course while your partner cheers you on. After you are both done, you can rearrange the course to create a new one together.

Variation: Time your child each time he does the obstacle course and see if he can beat his own time!

Tip: Vary the difficulty of the obstacle course depending upon your child's ability.

 Ball Pass

Challenge: Catching a ball

Motivation: Your child's specific motivations

How to Play: Take several cards and number each of them on one side. On the other side of each card, write a fun activity idea. Tape the cards to the wall, with the numbered side showing. Play catch with your child and count how many times you can pass the ball back and forth without dropping it. If you passed the ball 3 times, pick card #3 and do the activity written on the other side (like roll on the floor together or chase your child around the room until you catch him).

Tip: If your child has difficulty catching or throwing balls, start with a big ball (beach ball size) that is easy to grasp. As your child becomes more skilled, try using smaller balls.

Props:
- ❏ Ball
- ❏ Cards
- ❏ Tape

Notes:

219 Circus Show!

Challenge: Balancing objects on his head

Motivation: Anticipation, slapstick

How to Play: Come in dressed in a clown or circus costume and tell your child that you will be putting on a circus show for him. Have your child sit in a chair and show him several funny tricks that you can do while balancing a beanbag on your head (like walking on your toes or spinning slowly). If the beanbag falls off your head, do the trick again! Then ask your child to do a circus show with you by balancing the beanbag on his head while doing various tricks.

Props:
- ❏ Silly circus costume
- ❏ Beanbag (either store bought or homemade)

Notes:

220 Beanbag Toss

Challenge: Throwing

Motivation: Winning

How to Play: Tape two lines on the floor, leaving a distance of several feet between them. Explain to your child that one line indicates where to stand when throwing the beanbag and the other line indicates where to throw the beanbag. Give your child a beanbag and take one for yourself. Take turns standing on the first piece of tape and throwing the beanbag as close as possible to the second piece of tape on the floor without passing the line. The player whose beanbag got closest to the line (you may need to measure to determine with certainty) gets a point. The first person to get 5 points wins! Let your child know that the winner can request whatever he wants from the other person (e.g., a song, hug, dance or tickle) as his prize.

Props:
- ❏ 2 beanbags
- ❏ Pen
- ❏ Paper
- ❏ Tape

Notes:

Creative Closet Prop List

Crafts/art supplies:

- Decorative stickers
- Assorted beads (large or small depending on your child's skill level)
- String/shoelaces
- Paper
- Pen
- Child-sized scissors
- Tape
- Stapler
- Colored paper
- Oversized paper
- Pencil

Other:

- Laundry basket
- Laundry pins
- Assorted size bags with zippers, snaps and buttons
- Animal-shaped lacing boards
- Clothing-shaped lacing boards
- Colorful or decorative laces
- Play crown
- 3 bead containers

Fine Motor Games

⟨221⟩ Smelly Socks!

Props:
- ❐ Bag
- ❐ 5–10 socks
- ❐ Laundry basket
- ❐ Laundry pins

Notes:

Challenge: Pinching (laundry pins)

Motivation: Slapstick, being helpful

How to Play: Place 5–10 assorted socks into a bag located at one end of the room. Put a laundry basket into the other corner of the room. Tell your child that you have a bag of the dirtiest, smelliest socks and that they need to be put into the laundry right away—but they are way too smelly for you, so you need his help getting them into the laundry basket. Dump the bag of socks onto the floor and ask your child to help you by putting each sock into the basket. Explain to him that there is one condition—the socks are so dirty and smelly that he cannot even touch them with his fingers—each one needs to be picked up with a laundry pin and put into the laundry basket. Along the way, make dramatic faces about how stinky the socks are—you can even pretend to pass out!

⟨222⟩ New Shoes

Props:
- ❐ Pair of shoes
- ❐ Laces

Notes:

Challenge: Lacing

Motivation: Slapstick, being helpful

How to Play: Remove the laces from a pair of shoes and bring the shoes and the laces into the playroom. Tell your child that you just bought a pair of new shoes, but that the laces are missing—so that every time you try to walk in them, you trip and fall. Put on the shoes and demonstrate walking and then falling in an exaggerated way. Hand your child the laces and ask him to help by lacing up the shoes for you. It is not important that the shoes be laced properly—the goal is simply his getting the string into the hole. When the shoes are all laced up, try them on again, walk across the room and demonstrate how gracefully you can walk now (you can even do ballet leaps or jumping jacks!).

Tip: For a beginner, use shoes that have larger lacing holes. For a more advanced lacer, use shoes with smaller holes. You can also use colorful or decorative laces to make the game even more fun!

<223 Animal Surgery

Challenge: Lacing

Motivation: Animals, being helpful

How to Play: Fill a bag with animal-shaped lacing boards (these can either be bought at most toy stores or made by drawing animal shapes on cardboard and punching out holes on the periphery of the animal) and several laces. Tell your child that he is the "veterinarian" and that you need his help desperately! Show him an "animal" (lacing board) that got a big cut from falling out of a tree (or getting into a fight with another animal). Explain that the animal needs immediate surgery and needs to be sewn back up. Give your child the lace and have him sew away. When he is done, cheer and celebrate that the animal has now been healed!

Props:
- ☐ Bag
- ☐ Several animal-shaped lacing boards
- ☐ Several laces

Notes:

<224 Seamstress

Challenge: Lacing

Motivation: Being helpful, colorful laces

How to Play: Buy or make a clothing-shaped lacing board (in the shape of a dress, pants, etc.). Tell your child that you are going to a very important party or meeting and need your "clothes" to be sewn for this very important occasion. Ask your child to be the seamstress and help by sewing your clothes for you. Give your child the lace and have him sew away. When your child is done, thank him profusely and pretend to put on the clothes and go to a fancy party.

Props:
- ☐ Clothing-shaped lacing board
- ☐ Several colorful/decorative laces

Notes:

<225 Oh No, the Queen's Jewels!

Challenge: Picking up small objects, sorting

Motivation: Being helpful, organizing, beads

How to Play: Come into the room dressed as a queen or king. Wear a crown (bought or homemade) and carry a tray/plate containing assorted colored beads (e.g., red, blue and green). Tell your child that last night you tripped in the palace while you were holding your treasure box of jewels and that all of your jewels spilled out on the floor. The jewels are now a huge mess and need to be sorted into three groups (diamonds, rubies and emeralds). Color-code three containers by marking them with a colored sticker or by writing the color names on them. Ask your child to help you by sorting the beads into the appropriate containers.

Props:
- ☐ Crown
- ☐ Colored beads (3 different colors)
- ☐ Plate/tray
- ☐ 3 color-coded containers

Notes:

Variation: If the sorting seems too challenging, simply ask your child to help by picking up the beads and putting them all into the same container.

Tip: For a beginner, use larger beads since they are easier to handle.

✫226 The Queen's Crown

Props:
- ❏ Play crown
- ❏ 5–10 decorative stickers

Notes:

Challenge: Peeling and placing stickers

Motivation: Being helpful, stickers

How to Play: Come into the room dressed as a queen or king. Wear an undecorated crown (bought or homemade). Tell your child that all the jewels fell off your crown while you were riding home to your palace. Explain that you need his help putting the jewels back on. Give your child a sheet of 5–10 decorative stickers and ask him to put each "jewel" back on the crown. When your child is done, thank him profusely and model your new crown, or appoint your child as the new king and put the newly decorated crown on his head.

Variation: You can increase the challenge by drawing empty circles on the crown and asking your child to put the jewels onto those specific spots. Use bigger or smaller stickers depending upon your child's skill level.

✫227 Find the Hidden Treasure

Props:
- ❏ 4–5 different sized bags with buttons
- ❏ Zippers and snaps
- ❏ Small treasure item

Notes:

Challenge: Undoing buttons, zippers and snaps

Motivation: Finding a secret treasure

How to Play: Choose several bags that have buttons, zippers or snaps. Make sure that the bags range in size from large to small. Take the biggest bag and place a smaller bag inside. Inside the smaller bag, place an even smaller bag and continue with progressively smaller bags. In the smallest bag put a treasure. The treasure can be any small motivating item, such as a shiny coin, seashell or sparkly gem/rock. Close each bag. Explain to your child that a treasure is hidden inside the bag, and ask for his help in finding it. Have your child unbutton, unzip, unsnap each bag until he finally reaches the innermost bag—and the treasure!

☆228 I Can Dress Up All by Myself!

Challenge: Buttoning, zipping, fastening, snapping

Motivation: Dressing up, independence

How to Play: Fill a bag with clothes from members of your family (e.g., Daddy's button-down shirt/work shoes, a big sister's zippered sweatshirt/special belt). Tell your child that he will have the chance to dress up like someone else in the family. Have your child pick a family member. Give him the clothing of the person he chose and let him do the buttoning, zipping and snapping as independently as possible!

Variation: For additional motivation, tell your child that you will be his fashion photographer! Take a picture of your child dressed up as each family member and let him show it to that person later!

Props:
❏ Bag of dress-up clothes with buttons
❏ Zippers or snaps

Notes:

☆229 Friendship Necklace

Challenge: Stringing beads

Motivation: Colorful beads, giving a present to a friend

How to Play: Fill a box with beads (larger beads for a beginner and smaller beads for a child with more advanced skills) and a string. Ask your child to pick a friend or family member to whom he would like to give a special friendship necklace. Have him string the necklace with as little assistance as possible. When your child is done, ask him what he likes about that special friend and encourage him to relate his feelings to the friend when he gives him the necklace.

Props:
❏ Box
❏ Beads of assorted sizes
❏ String/lace

Notes:

☆230 Alphabet/Number Strips

Challenge: Cutting straight lines

Motivation: Making letters/numbers

How to Play: Draw lines on several pieces of paper. Give your child a pair of child-sized scissors and ask him to cut the lines in order to make strips. After your child has cut several strips, attach them using tape, stickers or a stapler, and create some of your child's favorite letters or numbers.

Props:
❏ Paper
❏ Pen
❏ Child-sized scissors
❏ Tape/stickers/stapler

Notes:

⟨231 The Chain Game

Props:

☐ 5–6 sheets of colored paper
☐ Child-sized scissors
☐ Stapler

Notes:

Challenge: Cutting straight lines

Motivation: Making a long chain

How to Play: Draw lines down the length of several sheets of colored paper. Ask your child to cut on the lines in order to make paper strips. Staple together the two ends of the first strip so that you have a loop. Put the next strip through the first loop and staple the ends of that strip in the same way. Continue until you have made a chain that you can hang in your house or use as a surprise decoration for another member of the family.

Variation: For a more easily attainable result, simply staple the strips to each other without looping them. See if you can make a line that reaches from one end of the room to the other.

⟨232 Balloon Decorations

Props:

☐ 5–6 sheets of colored paper
☐ Child-sized scissors
☐ Tape
☐ String

Notes:

Challenge: Cutting circles

Motivation: Being helpful, decorating the house

How to Play: Draw large circles on several sheets of colored paper. Tell your child that you will be decorating the house and that you need his help in preparing the balloons. Ask him to cut out the "balloon" circles on each page. When he has finished cutting, have him help you tape a piece of string onto the back of each balloon. Work together to tape the balloons all over the walls of any room you choose. Use the decorated room to have a pretend birthday for a doll or a celebratory dinner for the family!

⟨233⟩ The Amazing Maze

Challenge: Drawing within lines, holding a pen

Motivation: Reaching one of his favorite things

How to Play: Create a maze on an oversized piece of paper. Draw a picture of your child at the beginning of the maze and a picture of one of your child's favorite things (a car, a plate of pancakes or a friend that he loves) at the end of the maze. Label the "Start" and "Finish" points on the maze and show it to your child. Ask him to draw the path from the "Start" to the "Finish" in order to get to his favorite object.

Tip: For a beginner, create a wide maze path. For a child with more advanced skills, make the maze path narrower.

Variation: You can also direct your child to draw with a washable marker on a large mirror. Make it clear to your child that we do not draw on all mirrors or walls, but only this special "drawing mirror."

Props:
❑ Over-sized paper
❑ Thick pen

Notes:

⟨234⟩ Hidden Picture

Challenge: Drawing lines, holding a pen

Motivation: Discovering a picture of his favorite object

How to Play: Make a numbered dot-to-dot picture of one of your child's favorite things (dot-to-dot picture books can also be purchased at most toy stores—make sure that the pictures appeal to your child's interests). Number each dot in order of how to form the picture. Tell your child that there is a hidden picture within the dots. Ask him to connect the dots to discover what the picture is!

Tip: If your child is not familiar with numbers in sequence, you can make each dot a different color and then tell your child, "Now, draw a line from the yellow to the green!"

Variation: You can also direct your child to draw with a washable marker on a large mirror. Make it clear to your child that we do not draw on all mirrors or walls, but only this special "drawing mirror."

Props:
❑ Paper
❑ Pen

Notes:

⟨235 Help Me Find My Twin!

Props:

❏ Paper
❏ Pencil/pen

Notes:

Challenge: Holding a pen, copying pictures, drawing straight and curved lines, drawing circles

Motivation: Completing a matching picture

How to Play: Make a simple drawing of a family member or of one of your child's friends. Draw another copy, but leave some features missing (i.e., missing curly hair, an ear, a shoe, etc.). Explain to your child that the two drawings depict twins, but that they cannot find each other because they do not look alike. Ask your child to complete the picture with missing parts in order to help the twins find each other! Focus on having your child draw straight lines (arms and legs), curved lines (ears and mouth) or circles (eyes, nose and buttons on shirt). When the drawings have been matched, enact a dramatic reunion of the twins!

Tip: Play several rounds of this game. Start off by making the drawing challenge easier (only one missing feature) and gradually increase the difficulty level (several missing features), depending on your child's ability.

Appendix A

Additional Strategies for Critical Areas of Growth

Since the original publication of *Play to Grow!* in 2008, I have learned a tremendous amount as a professional in the autism field. Thanks to the hundreds of families I have worked with and professionals I have learned from, my knowledge base has continued to deepen over the years.

I have contributed articles to important autism resources—such as the Generation Rescue blog and *The Autism File* magazine—as well as posted weekly blog articles on my own website. I have written about topics such as dealing with challenging behaviors (like hitting, biting, pulling hair), how to promote social skills, helping the child who also struggles with anxiety, and so much more. I am eager to share these concepts and strategies with you. In this Appendix A, I am including a collection of some of these articles so you can use these tools with your child or the child you work with.

Reminder: Since autism has been diagnosed predominantly in boys (in a striking 4:1 ratio), we decided to simplify the language by using the masculine "he" in the following articles. However, the strategies and concepts presented absolutely apply to boys and girls alike.

6 Steps for Boosting Your Child's Social Skills

Time and time again, parents have shared with me that one of the main questions that keeps them up at night is: "Will my child ever make a friend?" or "Will my child ever have the sense of love, acceptance and belonging that comes from true friendship?"

In my work with families of children with autism since 1997, I have had the true honor and privilege of witnessing just that: children going from having no interest and ability in interacting, to playing with delight (both with their peers and other family members) and cultivating meaningful friendships.

My life's work is to help children, including yours, share his unique self with the world around him through meaningful and nurturing relationships.

After working with hundreds of children from around the world, I have seen that there are six steps, that when implemented, will cultivate success in your child's social skill development.

Though theory can be interesting, I'm all about giving you tools you can implement. So, beneath each step you will also see an "action step." This way, you know what to do and HOW to do it.

Are you ready to get started? Read on!

1. Prioritize Interaction (with YOU)

Now, this might seem simple, but you may be amazed at how frequently this is overlooked. Often, parents and professionals focus on skill acquisition; matching, building blocks, completing tasks, etc.

I'm not saying that these skills are not important, but I *am* saying that the focus on these skills often dominates. The skill of having natural and meaningful interaction with another person (which, in my experience, is the *core* challenge for anyone on the autism spectrum) is not given the attention it deserves.

It's time to tip the scale and prioritize interaction!

Your child interacting with you in fun and playful ways will not only enhance his relationship skills with you but will also create the foundation for him to transfer that desire and ability with his peers. But how do you do it?

Action Step: Create focused playtime, ideally 4–5 days a week (even 20 minutes at a time), where you are playing with your child in the activities he loves most. Remember, this is not time devoted to acquiring a specific skill but time dedicated for you and your child to delight in being together in a relationship.

This is a very important seed you are planting—one that is critical in growing your child's desire for friendship.

2. Minimize Sensory Overload

Let me create some context here: most of us have amazingly well-organized sensory systems that allow us to filter most stimuli so we can focus on what we are doing. Many children and adults on the autism spectrum have sensory processing disorders—often causing sensory overload.

A huge amount of energy is occupied with coping, organizing and shutting out stimuli, leaving little energy left for your child to learn, grow and socialize. Creating a nondistracting environment where you can prioritize interaction (Step 1) will make a *big* difference. This way your child can free up the energy he usually uses to just *manage* his sensory system and instead use his energy to interact with you!

Action Step: Find a room in your home (this can be your child's bedroom or a spare room) and clear out any major distractions, such as unnecessary toys, clutter, electronics, etc. Leave your phone outside (that's right!) and shut the door. Play one-on-one with your child and prioritize interaction in this safe and calming environment.

But *how* should you play? Keep reading…

3. Follow Your Child's Interest

Often parents are taught to limit or even avoid a child's interest or motivation and focus on more "socially appropriate interests." I suggest the opposite—see where your child is most lit up and use it as a doorway to help your child engage with you. Spend time doing what he loves to do with a sincere curiosity and desire to connect, even if that means lining up cars or drawing the same pictures over and over again. By doing this, your child can experience the confidence and strength of being on "his playing field" and will be more willing to do what is challenging—engaging with you. Meet your child where he is, and he will move toward you.

Plus, the look on your child's face when he sees that *finally* someone is doing what he loves to do is priceless.

Action Step: When you are playing one-to-one with your child in a non-distracting setting (Steps 1 and 2), observe carefully. See what your child is doing and do it too (and don't hold back—really get into it and have fun!).

4. Create Stepping Stone Skills

Often parents or professionals pursue the complex skill of making a friend without identifying and focusing on the incremental skills needed to achieve that broader goal. I call these "stepping stone skills."

This allows your child to be more easily successful and therefore a more confident and willing learner. As I often say, "Success builds confidence, and confidence builds more success."

The additional benefit is that you are more likely to see progress when focusing on smaller steps. The excitement in seeing this progress fuels stamina on your journey with your child.

Here are some examples of stepping stone skills you can focus on for making friends:

- Willingness to be around others
- Observing what others are doing
- Imitating what others are doing
- Going up to/joining others in activity
- Participating in an activity
- Staying in that activity for a period of time
- Adding his own ideas/direction in a game

Action Step: Identify what "stepping stone skill" you want to both observe and focus on for your child. (Steps 5 and 6 focus on how to develop those specific skills.)

5. Develop an Awareness of Peers

Before we even begin the entry into the world of peers, it is important that your child notices them and how they play/interact to begin with. Doing this takes all the pressure off your child to participate and just gives him a chance to observe while you point out the fun and benefit of playing with a friend.

By helping your child bring his attention to what peers are doing and how they are doing it, you allow your child to learn how social interaction works first.

Action Step: You can do this by taking your child to the park (on a day/time when it is quieter so he is less likely to get overwhelmed by all the commotion) and simply point out how the children are playing together.

For example: "Look! That boy is running and that girl is chasing him." Describe it in ways that may be interesting for your child, like, "Ooooo, look at that. She is fast! I think she's gonna catch him!"

6. Cultivate Intimate Social Experiences

Over the years I have had many opportunities to observe children in a school setting, and I am amazed, time and time again, how few opportunities there are for social skill development. The school day is very task oriented and full with directed learning. Plus, the classroom environment can be very hectic, making it almost impossible for your child to notice and take advantage of social opportunities.

For this reason, Step 6 is about turning down the volume on sensory overload and cultivating more *intimate* social experiences.

A great way to do this is **home play dates**: inviting a child (this can be a family member, the child of a friend of yours or someone from your child's school or afterschool activities) to your home for a 1- to 2-hour play date. The play date should consist of an activity facilitated by you (to give them both a specific framework) and some free play time.

The benefits of a home play date is that it is in your home environment (where your child is most comfortable) and allows your child the opportunity to develop a more intimate relationship with one child without having to manage the sensory overload of a *group* of children (plus, you have the control of choosing the child who might make a good match).

Action Step: Create a list of play date candidates and select 1–2 kids that you would like to invite.

Bonus Tip: Parent's often ask me, "Should I tell the parents of the child I want to invite over to a play date that my child has autism?" Well, this is really up to you and depends on how well you know the family. Overall, I suggest something like this: "I would love to invite Alex to our house to play. My son really loves him and he has challenges making friends, so I thought it would be a great way for him to develop his friendship skills. Would you be interested in setting up a play date at my house?"

There you have it, the "The 6 Steps to Boosting Your Child's Social Skills."

Now, I know how easy it can be to go into overwhelm, which leads to paralysis, and the next thing you know, you are not able to implement anything. So pick one step that you really want to focus on. Experiment with that one and observe how your child responds. You can always come back and pick up another step when you are ready.

Of course, these are no magic bullets, only perspectives and strategies that require consistent implementation. If you proceed, one step at a time, you are on your way to boosting your child's social skills and helping him bring his unique personality to the world around him.

Plus, by focusing on relationship building, you offer your child the most meaningful gift: the sense of love, acceptance and belonging that comes from true friendship.

Here is a success story I want to share with you.

There is nothing more inspiring than hearing about incredible growth from children who may have the same challenges that yours has. By hearing what is possible for one child, you can get a real sense of what can be possible for yours. So, let me share what one of my private coaching clients has witnessed with her own son Gilad in the past year.

When this mom came to me, she knew her child had boundless potential, but the therapies he was doing just weren't making the impact she was hoping for. She created a home-based play program, including implementing the "6 Steps" in playing with her son. He went from:

- Crying continually (70% of his play sessions was crying) to barely crying at all anymore

- Sporadically using one word to now using 3- to 4-word sentences (plus answering a variety of questions, asking questions and making comments in conversation)

- An attention span of 1–2 minutes to hours a time
- Having no interest in imaginary play to playing with pretend food, toy phones, etc.

Now he joins play and seeks out children both at the park and at school. And it is this that is most exciting for his mother (and me) to witness.

Gilad's story is a great reminder that connection and relationship is not only a critical goal in it of itself. It is also the means to cultivating other important life skills. When skills are taught in the context of play and connection, they become more meaningful, spontaneous and lasting for the child.

Put an End to Challenging Behaviors: Hitting, Biting, Throwing and More

Ibet you are you are reading this article right now because you feel like your life is ruled by putting out fires. In fact, you probably skipped right to this page with a feeling of desperation—anything to help my child stop hitting/biting/throwing! This is exactly why I decided to cover this topic today. Families who want to help their children with challenging behaviors want help *now!*

Plus, as you probably know, these kinds of behaviors affect the whole family, creating an element of stress that permeates the entire home. Implementing strategies to help your child move through these behaviors will not only hugely impact your special child but your whole family.

If you've got a "thrower/biter/hair puller," you know the huge amount of energy that is spent managing these behaviors, leaving little energy left for you or your child to focus on interaction, learning and other life skills. Plus, these kinds of behaviors bring your child a lot of negative attention.

The time to turn this all around is now so that you can experience more harmony in your home and see your child actualize his potential in every other area.

At this point, you are probably ready to race ahead and get those strategies, but wait a minute! Before we focus on what to do, I want to focus on what I call your "come from." Where are you coming from while you implement the strategies I am about to teach you? Before you implement any action, step one is to get your attitude in place so your action steps will be powerful and effective.

Here's how: before you are about to respond to your child's challenging behavior, STOP and take a step away. Take a moment and shift to a place of curiosity and actually excitement (I know that might sound crazy) about the fact that there is a teaching opportunity here. This is the moment where you can teach your child alternative ways to navigate through life with more success.

You want to come from a place of curiosity… "Why is my child biting/throwing/scratching?" Getting to the "why" will help you have compassion and understanding and implement targeted strategies that address the core issue and that will result in lasting change.

So… why is your child biting/throwing/scratching? There are the three main reasons why your child might be exhibiting a challenging behavior: to get a reaction, to take care of a bio-medical or sensory need, or to try and get what he wants. Let me explain these reasons a bit more.

Reason #1: Get a Reaction

Your child is trying to get a reaction from you, not because your child is malicious but simply because your reaction (getting red in the face, using a higher pitched voice, racing across the room to save the eggs from being dumped on floor) is exciting. Knowing that he can elicit this reaction from you, time and time again, gives your child a sense of control. Having control is incredibly exciting for children on the autism spectrum since they often experience a lack of control.

The predictability of "I throw eggs = Mommy screams" is exactly the kind of predictability your child may be looking for.

Reason # 2: Take Care of Himself

Often challenging behaviors is your child's way of taking care of a bio-medical or sensory need, such as: relieving pressure in his head (head banging, crashing into things), inflammation in his digestive track (hitting/screaming/self-injurious behavior), or calming an overactive sensory system or exciting an underactive sensory system (banging head, self-injurious activities, etc.).

Reason #3: Get What He Wants

Biting or hitting can be your child's way of trying to get something he wants: food, TV, iPhone, anything! Let's be honest—it often works, and even if it works 1 out of 10 times, it's worth trying again.

You want to be curious about which reason is driving your child's behavior and excited to help him learn a more effective way to handle any one of these situations.

Now, I am sure you are wondering, "How do I know which cause is driving my child's behavior?"

You discover this by implementing what I'm about to teach you (the 4 R's) and see which one works over time.

Here are four "R" strategies to help put an end to these challenging behaviors:

Strategy #1: React

Your reaction is crucial in helping your child move through any behavior. You want to think "act like a turtle"—slow and easy. You can do this by moving slowly, having a relaxed face and speaking with a level voice (even a drop lower than you usually speak). If your child is doing his behavior to get big reactions (reason #1), then eliminating the pay off, consistently over time, is your best bet at eliminating that behavior.

If your child is doing his behavior as a way to address a bio-medical or sensory need, you want to try addressing his sensory need in another way (I will get to that in strategy #2). But you want to be calm anyway. This will help you be more creative and not allow a behavior driven by a sensory need to result in the additional benefit of getting a big reaction. This will only exacerbate the behavior—which is the *last* thing you want to do.

If your child is biting/hitting to get what he wants and he sees over time that it does not work for him, then you are on your way to moving through that behavior.

No matter what reason is driving your child's behavior, responding in a slow and easy way will help take the payoff out of any behavior and decrease your child's desire to continue in this way.

Important Note: Consistency is critical here. Make sure to share these strategies with family and team members so you can help your child shift as quickly and easily as possible.

Strategy #2: Redirect

Redirect your child's sensory or bio-medical need into a more effective and more socially appropriate channel.

Oftentimes, behaviors are driven by your child's need to organize his sensory system. His sensory system might be overwhelmed and frazzled, or he may be trying to relieve pressure or discomfort. Your child is not bad; he is simply trying to take care of himself. For example, if your child is biting (biting themselves, other people, or his shirt), then he clearly has a need to bite. You can say, calmly and easily, "I see you are biting. Let me help you have something to bite without hurting yourself or others."

Then offer your child an alternative. Here is a list of some alternatives to the most common challenging behaviors:

- Biting: a sensory box with special chewy toys
- Hitting: bean bag, punching bag
- Jumping: trampoline, climbing equipment
- Banging head: deep head squeezes
- Throwing: balls/bean bags

The message you are giving your child is: "It's OK if you have this need. I want to help you address this need in an effective way that won't hurt me, yourself or others." This way, while addressing your child's behavior you are also conveying love, compassion and acceptance of your child. The result is not only a shift in behavior but a deepening in your relationship with your child.

Strategy #3: Recover

Uncover and recover your child's bio-medical needs to address things like yeast overgrowth, metal toxicity and digestive problems. By using a variety of therapies—such as diet intervention, homeopathy and/or cranial sacral therapy—you address the root cause of behavior. This is an extensive journey, but your persistence will pay off!

Strategy #4: Respond

As I mentioned in Strategy #1, you want to give as little reaction as possible to all the things your child is doing that you'd like to decrease or eliminate.

But there is a flip side. You want to give a very enthusiastic response to all the things you'd like to encourage, such as, touching gently, using alternatives (like biting a toy versus himself) or communicating (versus screaming).

The basic concept is this: if your child sees consistently that crying/screaming/hitting does not get him what he wants or get him a big reaction *BUT* that communicating with words or being gentle does, then he will naturally move toward those things more often.

Bonus Point: Make your life easier by adapting your environment so your child does not have the same ease and access to do his challenging behaviors.

For example, if your child likes to dump out eggs, put a lock on the fridge. If your child likes to flush things down the toilets, lock the toilet seats or the bathroom. If your child likes to climb shelves, put locked doors on your bookcases. Is this a Band-Aid approach? Yes. But it buys you time and makes life easier while you implement the four strategies to create deeper and more meaningful change.

You can do this. There is no magic here, but powerful strategies that allow you to put an end to feeling helpless and instead create a major shift in your child's behavior and in your family life as a whole.

Here's a success story I want to share with you.

How can implementing the four strategies make an impact with your child? Let me answer this by sharing a story about a one of my private coaching clients Allison and her son Joey. Joey was a "jumper." He used to constantly jump off furniture: dressers, bookcases and couches. Allison, who also had two other children with autism, would run around to make sure he would not get hurt (let alone damage the furniture). As you can imagine, this was exhausting for her and took up all of her energy.

She changed her reaction (Strategy #1) from running and screaming to moving slowly and calmly. She redirected his sensory need (Strategy #2) and invested in a trampoline and outdoor climbing equipment. She worked to recover his digestive system (Strategy #3) by implementing a cleaner diet. She responded with enthusiasm (Strategy #4) when he jumped from the playground equipment instead, *and* she adapted her environment (Bonus Point) and locked all the bedroom doors that had a high dresser he could jump off.

Allison saw a huge decrease in Joey's jumping. He is now able to grow in so many other areas, and now he receives tons of positive attention versus constant discipline. Plus, with a huge decrease in the level of stress in the house, every single member of the family has a more peaceful environment and Allison is much more able to be present with Joey and her other children.

6 Strategies to Help Your Child Move Through Anxiety

Just yesterday I shared an article on Facebook about how to help your child with anxiety, and it was shared over 158 times in less than 24 hours. This let me know how important an issue this is for many families out there, and so I wanted to addresses autism and anxiety further here today.

Your child may have anxiety over a variety of issues: sounds, social situations, going to bed, the dark or something very specific like car washes. I worked with a child who had a panic attack every time her mother drove past a sign for a car wash.

No matter what your child is feeling anxious about, below are some key strategies you can implement to help soothe anxiety and help your child navigate through life with more ease and confidence.

1. Identify Your Child's Anxiety

Your child may express anxiety in a variety of ways. He might tell you directly that he is fearful or anxious about something, or you might see an increase in intensity of stimming (flapping, head banging, verbal stims, etc.). It's important to stop and recognize that your child is not trying to be difficult or stubborn but instead is having an incredibly challenging time coping with the situation. If you come from a place of understanding and compassion, you will be much more able to facilitate your child through it.

2. Create an Anxiety Log

Sometimes it may seem that your child escalates his screeching/biting/ tantrums out of nowhere. However, if you make a log and record when you see your child showing behaviors that might indicate he is feeling anxious, a pattern may emerge and help you be much more targeted in addressing the challenge (for example, whenever a particular person comes to the house, about 20 minutes after lunch, before a particular therapy, at the grocery store, etc.).

3. Decrease the Sensory Overload

Time and time again people with autism have expressed the great anxiety they feel due to a disorganized sensory system, making seemingly simple things like a trip to the grocery store incredibly overwhelming. So this is an important one: do your best to *decrease* the sensory overload your child might experience. You can do this by either eliminating/limiting or modifying trips to stimulating environments. For example, don't take your child grocery shopping (or the park, etc.) for now, or take him much less often, or take him only on off hours, when it is much more quiet and less crowded. This is an important time to be an open-minded detective because something that may not seem stimulating to you can be incredibly challenging for your child.

4. Create a Sensory Haven

No matter how much sensory input you try to manage, your child still might experience an aspect of overwhelm, and so creating a quiet and safe place where you child can unwind is very important. You can use your child's bedroom, or a corner of a room, that has toys and supplies that may help your child unwind, for example, bean bags to sit in, squeeze toys, a weighted blanket, their favorite stim toys, etc.

5. Be the "Calm in the Storm"

Children with autism—especially children who do not yet use words to communicate—are very sensitive to how we are feeling and will often pick up on and respond to the slightest stress we may feel. You cannot "mask" this from your child, as you probably know. So, especially when your child seems anxious, be aware of how you are feeling and shift to a place of calm. (You can do this by stepping out of the situation and taking five slow breaths; count as you breathe and notice how it feels in your body). As I often say, "Be the change that you want to see in your child."

6. Calm the Body

Nothing is more organizing for a child than giving him deep, calming squeezes. Time and time again, families I work with have implemented deep squeezes in the arms, head, hands, and feet, and the temper tantrums decrease almost instantly. Many children will also begin to ask for these deep squeezes as they experience how much it helps them feel more calm and organized. Experiment with what works best for your child, and offer squeezes before and during times when your child may be anxious.

Additional Suggestions

Over the years I have discovered—both with my own children and families that I work—many wonderful ways to support a child in feeling less anxious. Here are a few:

- Essential oils
- Bach flower remedies
- Homeopathy
- Music

☆ Making the Holidays Work for Your Child

Octover has begun and the parade of holidays is upon us: Halloween, Thanksgiving, Hanukkah and Christmas are all around the corner.

Many families I work with experience a heightened level of challenge with their child on the autism spectrum during holiday season.

- Big family gatherings can be stressful (and result in meltdowns).

- Exposure to foods not on your child's diet can be stressful (and result in meltdowns).

- A lack of structure and predictable routine can be stressful (and result in meltdowns).

The bottom line is that for a child who has a sensory processing disorder, social challenges/anxiety, bio-medical digestive issues, and a need for a calm and predictable routine, the holidays can be a time of heightened challenge for the whole family.

Just last week I had the honor of attending the bar-mitzvah (a Jewish "coming of age" ritual for boys when they turn 13) for a boy named Shmuel, whom I had worked with for many years. Being at Shmuel's bar-mitzvah was incredibly meaningful for me as I watched him sit at the head table, sing a song while holding his father's hand, and dance in a circle with other adolescents from his school with a beaming face. It was also one of the most successful events for a child with autism I had ever experienced.

I want to share with you some key components that really made this family/community event work so that you can help make the holidays work for your child and family as well:

1. Small and Simple

A gathering of your family/friends does not have to be a huge and wild event. Try spending the holidays with your close family and friends (especially those folks who accept your child and your parenting versus those who judge you and your child). This will help prevent sensory overload for your child. You might consider hosting a family gathering (so your child feels most comfortable), and everyone can help so you are not overwhelmed doing all the cooking/cleaning! This also gives you more control over what food will or will not be there for a child on a special diet.

2. Give Your Child a Role

One of the things that made the bar-mitzvah so successful was that Shmuel sat at a designated table and had activities to engage in (dancing with his friends, singing songs, eating, etc.) Maybe your child is not willing to go trick-or-treating on Halloween, but he might love the job of passing out the treats to all the visitors (I loved doing this when I was a kid!). Or maybe he'd enjoy passing out the presents on Hanukkah or Christmas.

3. Create Predictability As Much As Possible

For example, show your child pictures of who will be attending a family gathering or pictures of what will be happening (first you will get into costumes, then friends will come over, then you will go from house to house, then you will come home and sort through the goody bag, etc.) The more your child can know what to expect, the more relaxed he can be and enjoy the holiday activity.

4. Give Your Child a "Way Out"

If the gathering becomes too chaotic for your child, let him know ahead of time that he can go to a quiet place (like his bedroom) and play there with activities that are soothing for him (puzzles, blocks, books, etc.). Have his room set up with these activities so he can independently self-soothe while the party is in action.

However, more important than all of these steps is your mindset. Often when cousins (especially those your child's age) get together, parents begin to compare their child to others, and your child's challenges might seem more pronounced. Set yourself up and decide to use the holidays to celebrate—both who your child is and the seemingly "small" steps he is making on his journey. He may not be willing to squeeze into a vampire costume, but maybe he is willing to wear a hat; that is worth celebrating. He might not be ready to engage with his cousins, but he may let them use his favorite toy or sit beside them while they play.

Honor these moments, because these are your gifts and you don't want to miss them. You deserve them.

☆ Utilizing (Versus Minimizing) Your Child's Differences

Have you ever heard the term "trying to close the gap"? This is a term I hear often, and it refers to closing the gap between a special child and his peers. While I certainly support the idea of helping every child to be able to fully integrate and succeed with other children his age, I think the goal of "closing the gap" poses a particular problem. With this goal in mind and with the best intentions in the world, parents may try to minimize the differences between their child and other children.

I am here to make a stand for a different goal.

Instead of focusing on minimizing the differences, what if we focused on identifying and utilizing differences as a way to help each child actualize his own unique potential. What this means is shifting your focus from trying to help your child be just like all the others to helping your child more fully bring his unique self to the world around him.

This may seem like a subtle shift in focus, but the impact can be profound.

Doing this allows your child to flourish in a way that is unique to him and, in my experience, children are more inspired to grow when they are truly "seen." So, not only does it feel better for you and your child, but it also promotes deeper and more meaningful growth.

You might be thinking, "This sounds great theoretically, but how do I identify and utilize my child's differences to help her have optimal growth?"

Great question! Read below for some key ways to do this:

1. Learning Style

Many children on the autism spectrum have a delay in audio processing and are stronger visual learners. By identifying and utilizing this learning style (versus trying to minimize it), you can help your child learn by using more visual strategies. For example, use picture/word cards as you explain to your child what will be happening that day or describe new concepts or complex social situations. Most of us are visual learners. I have to see a new word in the dictionary in order for me to remember it; hearing it is not enough.Utilizing this difference can be critical in helping your child actualize his potential.

2. Learning Environment

Many children on the autism spectrum also have a sensory processing disorder, making it very difficult to filter out external stimulation. This can result in your child being easily overwhelmed in a highly stimulating environment. What typically happens is that your child is so busy managing his sensory system that he has very little energy left to learn or interact. By identifying and utilizing this difference, you can make choices about the environments that will help your child grow. For example, you can go to the local park/pool/mall during off hours when there are fewer children and less commotion. You can also spend one-on-one time with your child in a closed room during focused play/learning time. This down time can be like a sensory haven for your child and allow him to rest and put his energy into growing in other areas.

3. Unique Motivations

Your child might need a bit more inspiration to do what is challenging for him (such as learning cognitive skills, communicating, engaging in turn-taking games, etc.). You can help your child be motivated and engaged if the learning experience is grounded in his unique motivations. For example, if you are trying to teach your child counting or adding and he *loves* cars, use toy cars in a counting or adding game. If you are trying to help your child play simple turn-taking games and he *loves* dinosaurs, make a simple "memory" card game from dinosaur pictures you find on the Internet.

We all want to be loved and honored for our unique selves, and our children are no different. Something as seemingly small as shifting your intention with your child from "closing the gap" to "actualizing his own unique potential" can make a tremendous impact and allow you to identify and utilize what is unique about your child. Often, it is these very differences—the ones that are minimized when trying to "close the gap"—that are the very keys to your child's exponential growth.

☆ What Your Child Needs Most to Help Him Grow

I just finished watching a video of one of one of my private clients, Patty, playing with her son, Eric. What I saw was a devoted mother trying to help her child stay on task with a variety of activities: puzzles, matching cards and reading books.

She was working hard, and it looked like she was "trying to pull teeth."

Anytime there was physical contact, he began to giggle (the cutest giggle I have ever heard, by the way). Then he began throwing cards and tried to climb on her back.

I watched with interest, and it became very clear to me that I was not watching a child who was behaving "badly." I was watching a child who was seeking interaction. I was watching a child who wanted to be tickled and tossed, a child who wanted to play with his mom.

The funny thing is that I see this dynamic over and over again—a parent/therapist trying to get a child to stay on task and do an activity while the child wants to play. The child is told to stop being "silly" and stay on task.

You might say it is your job to help your child stay on task since that his where his skills will grow. But what if I told you that interactive play is what your child needs *most* to help him grow?

The core challenge with any child on the autism spectrum is *interaction,* and the single place your child will be willing to stretch himself most in acquiring specific skills is in the context of fun-based play with *you.*

So not only does focusing on interactive play help you return to the delightful parent-child relationship that might have gotten lost since the diagnosis, but it also creates the most powerful and meaningful context for your child to grow in his skills.

So how do you do it?

Here's how to cultivate fun based play that your child will both love and grow from:

1. Spend One-to-One Time with Your Child in a Distraction-Free Environment

Find a room in your home with the least distractions (this can be your child's bedroom). Make a commitment to spend 20 minutes, 3 times a week with your child in this room. Schedule this time in your calendar or it won't happen!

2. Create a Laser-Sharp Intention

This time with your child is not about getting your child to complete a task. This time is dedicated to cultivating the *connection*.

3. Go With (Not Against) Your Child's Interests

What makes your child light up? Does he love tickles, squeezes, balloons, bubbles, singing songs, bouncing on a ball? The more your child is motivated, the deeper the quality of the interaction will be. Identify what it is your child loves to do and do *that*— together. If you feel like you are pulling teeth, then that means you are not working with your child's motivations.

Once this fun, interactive play is created, you have achieved your primary goal: to offer your child the positive experience of being with people.

Not only that, once your child is motivated and present with you, you now have a child who is available to stretch himself: communicating (because he wants that tickle), participating (giving you the bubble wand so you can blow more bubbles), and following directions (doing the hand movements to some of his favorite songs you are singing).

However, these are your secondary goals. Without the fun-based interaction first, your child will simply not be available or motivated to stretch himself, and you are back to the same ole' pulling teeth routine.

As you and your child prepare for a new school year ahead, the goal of creating fun based interaction is more important than ever. School is often heavy-handed on the task-oriented skills. This is your opportunity to carve out time and focus on deepening your relationship with your child and his love of interacting with others.

It is from this relationship that all other skills will grow.

☆ Bringing the Hidden Miracles to Light

During Chanukah, the Jewish festival of lights, we light a candle each night, adding more light as the holiday progresses. To me, this holiday is about bringing to light the "hidden miracles" in our lives. These hidden miracles are the wondrous things in your life that you were not looking for, may not notice, or do not see as gifts.

In my work with parents of children with autism, I have noticed that parents often see their children with a very specific checklist in mind of goals and skills to achieve. Their "eyes are on the prize," searching desperately for signs that their child is moving in that direction (for example, beginning to produce verbal communication, showing interest in others, becoming interested in using the toilet, etc.).

Many of the parents I work with often watch their children like a hawk, dutifully tracking their child's progress in these areas.

Yes, there is tremendous value in having customized goals and tracking progress in those goals (in fact, this is the bulk of what I do with the families I work with). However, I have also noticed that when we are observing our children in this way, our vision becomes quite narrow.

The truth is, all you see is what you are specifically looking for.

When looking at your child with the lenses of growth in specific areas, you do not open yourself to the broader scope of ways your child might be growing or developing.

You might notice if your child has made a new sound or not, but you might not notice the way your child let his brother play with his favorite toy (versus pushing him away) or that he laughed appropriately at something you did not think he understood.

By looking at your child through a narrower, goal-oriented lens, you are not seeing child fully or experiencing him for who he is.

Plus, you may be missing out on exciting developments simply because you are not looking for them.

How do you use a wider lens to experience your child more fully?

The answer is the following simple, two-step process:

1. Ask a New Question

In addition to asking yourself, "Is my child making progress in_____?" (fill in the blank with the specific goal you are working on with your child), add one of the following questions as you start your day:

"What new aspect of my child will I discover today?"

"What new developments will I observe in my child today?"

Asking yourself a more open-ended question leaves you more open to experiencing your child in a broader way.

2. Be Open and Curious

Be open and curious as your day unfolds to see what new developments or aspects of his personality your child might reveal to you. Experience your child with open eyes and an open mind.

By doing this, as in the Festival of Lights, you will create an opportunity to bring to light the hidden miracles in your life with your child. In my experience, this will create a further intimacy in your relationship with your child as well as a deepened sense of wonder for who your child truly is (aside from the IEP's and checklists!).

☆ How to Help Your Child Join In

Why does your child with autism often stay on the side lines and not participate in activities or conversations with you or others? Let me answer this question by sharing a story with you.

Just last week I was watching a video of one of my private coaching clients and her daughter and this is what I saw:

The mother asked her daughter to bring some pretend food to the table to feed the dolls, and her daughter did not do it right away. The mother then moved on to get clothing for the dolls, and while she was dressing the dolls the daughter went and brought the food to the table. But the mom did not notice because she had moved on to dressing the dolls.

The mother then asked her daughter a question, and the daughter did not respond right away. Then her daughter answered the question, but the mother did not notice because she had moved on and was talking about something else.

And so on and so on….

What was actually happening was that the mother was working at one speed while her daughter was working at another speed all together, and so they kept missing each other.

Even more significant was the fact that the daughter was actually participating and responding, but the mother was going so quickly that she did not notice or acknowledge the ways her daughter was participating in play or conversation.

I explained this phenomenon with an analogy:

Remember those playground merry-go-rounds that you used to play on as a kid? If the merry-go-round is spinning too fast, you simply cannot jump on and join in. In fact, everything looks like a big blur.

However, if the merry-go-round is spinning at a slower rate so that you can see exactly where there is a place for you to jump in, then you can and do!

Often, we are moving at such a quick pace—so different than our children, who frequently have sensory processing delays—that it is nearly impossible for them to jump in and join in. We are simply a spinning blur.

In fact, a study done at the University of Texas noted unique brain wave patterns in autistic children that showed them processing sounds a fraction of a second more slowly than other children. That fraction of a second, when added up for each and every sound, can cascade into a major obstacle in understanding people. Imagine if it took you a tiny bit longer than normal to understand each syllable. By the end of a whole sentence you would be very confused!

Once you become aware of the pace at which your child works, learns and understands, the solution is actually quite simple:

1. Slow Down

2. Pause

Create clear pauses in your play or conversation so you child can join in, as long as a slow count to 5. This may seem like a dramatic pause for you, but it might be exactly what your child needs to join in.

3. Zip It

Talk less and leave more room for silence so your child has clear pockets of opportunities to join in.

These three simple steps allow you to slow down "the spinning blur of people" and cultivate clear opportunities for your child to grow, participate and contribute instead.

Where Does Your Child's Soul Shine?

I want to tell you a story that demonstrates something I feel very strongly about, both as a teacher and as a parent.

Not long ago I was speaking with a mom named Mary, who told me her son loved going to Saturday morning services at their local synagogue and singing songs with the congregation. It was the absolute highlight of his week.

With the best intentions, his main therapists advised Mary to no longer take him there because he would then continue to sing those songs throughout the week and it seemed to take his focus away from some of the learning tasks they were working on.

So, wanting to do what is best for her son, that's what Mary did. She no longer allowed her son to go to Saturday morning services … and you know what happened?

It was like the light turned off inside of him. His natural shine became dimmer, and though he may have done some of his learning tasks, he did them with no heart. Of course, his learning was superficial, and he was not able to generalize what he was learning.

I suggested that Mary take her son back to services to let him sing his heart out—because each person has a soul, and it is his soul we want to help him shine. This is his unique gift that he was meant to bring to this world.

And *then,* I explained further, she could use this as a medium to teach him all kinds of things: leadership in the community (by leading some of the songs in the congregation), reading (as he follows along with the songs he loves), following directions and being a part of a social group (as he moves through the order of the service with others), etc.

The list is endless.

So, that's what Mary did.

Several months later she wrote to me saying how much happier he is, how much more engaged he is, and how his love for these songs led him to a love for piano. And, to everyone's amazement, he recently performed at an autism charity event that his family held (talk about contributing to the community!).

Sometimes, in our desire to teach a child skills, we end up focusing on all the areas that are most challenging for that child, and what can begin to happen is that a child's natural delight and enthusiasm in the world (i.e., his shiny soul) can begin to dim.

But the truth is . . .

- It is this shiny soul that will drive all meaningful learning and growth for your child.

- It is this shiny soul that your child was meant to bring to this world (and I'll tell ya', the world needs it).

- It is this shiny soul that makes your child such an important member of your family.

- It is this shiny soul that wants to be seen.

And when you see/connect with and cultivate your child's shiny soul, your relationship with your child deepens in ways you never thought possible.

☆ How to Speak to Your Child (and Why It Even Matters)

Parents often focus on how their child is communicating (or not communicating) to them. However, what is given less attention is how to speak to your child with autism.

What do I mean and why does it matter?

Let me begin with this premise: Your child's comprehension has *nothing* to do with your child's verbal production.

If a child does not speak or speaks in limited ways (such as speaking to get his needs met but not to express feelings/experiences), it is sometimes assumed that a child's ability to understand communication is limited as well.

However, this is not true at all. We now know this based on many people with autism who are nonverbal but use typing to express the most insightful and eloquent thoughts and feelings.

This is why it is very important to speak to your child's true intelligence.

When you speak to your child's true intelligence, you communicate to your child that you *believe* in his ability to understand you, which will help build his sense of self-worth and confidence. This will also make communicating and participating with you and others much more attractive, because your child will feel "truly seen" for who he is.

Parents have shared with me that as they communicate this way with their child, they see an almost instant response. Their child seems to stand taller or have an expression on his face that communicates a satisfaction in being recognized for his true abilities.

So how do you do it?

Here are three ways to speak to your child's true intelligence:

1. Celebration/Acknowledgment

This is a place where I see parents, with the best intentions in the world, do "baby talk" with their kids. For example; using a babyish voice and clapping and cheering for your 9-year-old son when he put his pants on by himself.

Here is an alternative: "Hey, Jack, it is really incredible to see the ways you grow and change every day, like putting on your pants by yourself. You are so inspiring" (all said in a sincere, heartfelt tone, one that you would use when talking to your best friend).

2. Explain What You Are Doing and Why

Often times children are expected to participate in an activity without having any understanding as to why they are doing it.

Here is a perfect example: A parent I recently began working with told me that her daughter was fighting taking a supplement. We talked about the need to explain why they were giving it to her, such as, "Bella, we are giving you this supplement to help build your muscles so you can do things like walk and dance. I know how much you love to dance!"

Well, what do ya' know? She opened her mouth and took that supplement. There is no better way to get your child on board than explaining *why* in a way that matches what they want for themselves.

3. Emotive Expression

This is about simply opening your heart to your child. Here are some examples:

- "Ben, I just want you to know that I learn so much from you, especially about working hard at something. I am so blessed that you are my son."

- "I know it was tough at the birthday party today, and I totally understand why you wanted to leave. I hope you are feeling more calm and relaxed now that we are home."

- "It is incredible to watch you play piano. You are so skilled and passionate about your music."

- "I know that your body hurts. We are doing our best to find ways to help you, and we won't stop until we find them".

The examples are many; the point is that your child will feel and understand what you are communicating.

I have to add one thing to avoid: Avoid talking about your child in front of him. Just like speaking to your child's true intelligence communicates your belief in his abilities, speaking about him as if he were not there (when he really is) communicates just the opposite.

What is one other way you can speak to your child's true intelligence?

Is Your Child Regressing (and What Can You Do about It)?

I want to share a story with you about one of my private coaching clients from Australia named Rachael.

We had a consultation one month ago in which she described all the new and exciting developments her son Ryan was making. He was communicating more, interacting more, showed interest in toys and activities he didn't even notice before, and even joined in on a ball game at the park with a family he had never met before ("This totally blew us away!").

So, of course, we discussed specific strategies she could use to take this further and help this growth momentum continue and deepen.

In our follow up consultation, I asked her how it had been going, and she shared with me that a week after our last consultation, Ryan just shut down. His eye contact dropped, his exclusive play went up, and he began a bout of meltdowns (you know, those really fun ones smack in the middle of a toy store) that lasted about 2 to 3 weeks.

But Rachael knew something that I want to make sure you all know. What she knew is this: Growth often happens in a zig-zag pattern *and* consists of pockets (sometimes lasting several days to several weeks) of what may look like a regression but is actually what I call an "acclimatization."

Fancy word, I know, but what does it mean?

Let me explain by using the analogy of ascending a steep mountain. One of the big risks in climbing a mountain like Everest or Kilimanjaro is altitude sickness, which is caused by going too high too quickly (not giving your body the time that it needs to adjust to the new elevation).

If you look in any mountain climbing guide, you will see that one of the best treatments for altitude sickness is descent, or as climbers say, "Climb high and sleep low." (I actually did climb Mt. Kilimanjaro many years ago, and this is exactly what we did.)

So, when your child is ascending his mountain (which he is doing every single day, as are you), descending is a critical component to ascension.

Your child might have a decrease in communication/interaction/flexibility right before or right after a big ascension. This is his brilliant way of organizing his system so he can integrate the learning growth that just happened or prepare himself for the learning burst ahead.

What this means for you is that when you see your child "acclimating," you can actually be excited because you know something big is about to or just did happen (talk about flipping something on its head!).

This is in *no way* regression but instead the necessary path to the top (though it may look like coming down).

So what happened with Ryan?

He made an incredible ascension (as described above) and then listened to his body and acclimated (turned inward and organized all his growth).

What did Rachael and her team do? With the understanding of the need to acclimate, they were easy with him, followed his lead, took a break from challenging, and nurtured this place with patience.

And what happened next? After taking the time he needed, Ryan emerged. He is making more sounds than before, showing interests in even more activities, and engaging more full with his family and team.

Yes, his path to the top continued, every step of the way.

So don't be fooled or frightened by the period when your child is acclimating, since it may look that he has stopped growing or even lost skills he once had.

Instead, cultivate and nurture it, for it is a critical stage in your child's ultimate ascension to the top.

Appendix B: Taking Care of You

In my work with families with children on the autistic spectrum, I have seen many parents consistently neglect their own needs: health, relationships, creative/spiritual pursuits, etc.

It has become very clear to me that there is an urgent need to spread the message of self-care. This is critical for a number of reasons. Prioritizing taking care of yourself will help you avoid burn out and have the stamina you need to truly go the distance with your child instead. Self-care is also important to enhance the quality of your life because, quite simply, you deserve it.

It is for these reasons (and many more) that I have gathered this collection of my articles on the topic of self-care. I want to help you prioritize taking care of *you* on your autism journey.

⭐ Self-Care: 7 Steps to a More Rejuvenated You

In my experience working with families, I have seen that most parents are resistant to focusing on themselves.

Have you ever had these thoughts?

- "I cannot focus on myself right now. That will only take time away from helping my child."

- "I feel guilty focusing on myself. It feels so selfish"

- "The clock is ticking. I have to sink all my time into my child *now*, and I can take a vacation later."

As one of my clients put it, "I feel like I began running the day my son was diagnosed, and I haven't stopped since!"

For those of you who are a part of my global autism community, you probably know that I am on a mission to help children with autism actualize their potential. However, what you may not know is that this is only half of my mission. The other half is to help you—parents—prioritize self-care.

Here's why:

Your journey requires stamina. This is not a sprint; this is your life. Often parents get caught up with the notion of a quick recovery process: "It will take a year or two to put up with all the hard work and stress, and *then* I can enjoy a happy and satisfied life and take the dream vacation with my spouse."

But, as you probably know by now, it does not work that way. No one knows how long this journey will take, but without question your journey with your child requires stamina and persistence. (This is true not just for parents of a special child but for parents in general!)

What do you risk by not prioritizing self-care? If you continue to ignore your own needs, you will eventually burn out and will be of no use to anyone. This is why self-care is #1 in your mission of helping your child.

Be a model to your children. When you prioritize taking care of yourself, you become a model to your family. Your actions will express the idea that "I value who I am. I value my needs/wants." Doing this will not only help your family value *your* needs/wants but it will make you a model for the value of taking care of themselves (such as taking alone time when they need it).

Enhance the quality of your life. You are more than a parent of a child with autism. You are beyond all your roles in life (mother/father/son/daughter/wife/husband/etc.). Remembering who *you* are is essential in bringing balance back into your life.

You might be asking, What am I beyond a parent to a person with autism? Who was I before autism came into my life? Who am I now? It is forgetting these things that brings a lack of balance—and it is this balance that I hope to bring back into focus.

But, how do you do this? I have a system called the "Wheel of Life" that I use with my private coaching clients that will help you reflect on all aspects of your life and make the decision to focus and attend to the areas that matter most to you so that you can fill *your own* tank.

For the purpose of this article, I am going to select the top three areas in life that are both the most important to parents yet often the most neglected, together with my seven steps to a more rejuvenated you:

Relationships (Primary/Family/Social)

This has to do with your relationships with your spouse, partner, other family members or friends. This area of life is so important because relationships are nurturing and supportive—who couldn't use more support and nurturing? Yet it is also the area most often shoved aside in the name of "Who has time for that now? … I've got to focus solely on my child."

Without nurturing and support, you can go only so far before you will crack, burn out or resent your child and your journey with him or her.

If this area feels neglected in your life, here is step #1 to turn that around:

1. Schedule a weekly date. This can be with your partner, best friend, sister, etc. It can be as little as 45 minutes at a coffee shop or a 30-minute walk. This is time to spend with those who love you and do not judge you or your child, so select this person carefully, otherwise your time together will be anything but nurturing. The key element is that is must be scheduled or else it won't happen. Carve out the time and work everything else around that schedule.

Wellness
(Physical Health/Fitness/Mental and
Emotional Health/Spiritual Growth)

Yes, I know this covers a lot of areas, but wellness truly is an integrated sector that touches upon body, mind, heart and soul. I have worked with parents who have neglected some serious health issues, become lethargic and overweight, become anxious and depressed, or never took the time to take care of themselves. Again, it's only a matter of time before you can no longer go on like this.

So, here are some ways to prioritize wellness:

2. Exercise. There is nothing more invigorating than moving your body, releasing stress and getting your blood circulating. This can be done in a variety of ways, like taking a yoga, aerobics or even kick boxing class. I have a client who joined a running group, and she loves it! Plus, joining a class or group has the added benefit of incorporating a social element to your exercise.

3. Diet. By diet I mean committing to how/what you eat in one way that will help you have more energy, clarity and balance. Several parents I work with decided to remove wheat or sugar from their diets and experienced a great change. Think about what aspect of your diet you would most like to change by either removing something, like processed sugar, or adding something, like more water or fresh vegetables.

4. Seek professional support. This can come in so many ways, like making a weekly appointment for massage or acupuncture or visiting a nutritionist or therapist. Though it may seem incredibly indulgent, it is really about what you need to do to be your best self—for you and your family—than a luxury.

5. Create a spiritual practice. Again, this can be in a million different ways: daily meditation, going to church or temple on a weekly basis, spending reflective time in nature. This will not only fulfill your spiritual needs, but it can also be a great social outlet.

Rejuvenation
(Rest/Nurturing Activities/Alone Time)

Now, I know what you may be thinking: Alone time? Yeah, I get alone time . . . when I'm on the toilet!

Many of you are incredibly sleep deprived and barely have a second to yourself to unwind and get centered. Remember that the less balanced you are, the less present and patient you are for your family.

Here are some ways to create more rejuvenation:

6. Sleep. Getting to bed earlier can make a huge difference in your day. Create a very specific schedule to get you in bed one hour earlier than you currently are. Once you are in bed, this is not the time to read the latest research on autism treatments. It is the time to read for pleasure or to give yourself a foot massage by candlelight.

7. Get some alone time. This can be a 30-minute bath, getting back into your painting (I have a client who sends me pictures of her newest painting projects), a daily morning walk, or even a getaway (by yourself or with girlfriends).

There are endless ways to prioritize self-care in your life. The important message I am trying to convey is to *make it a priority.* Because if you don't, nobody else will.

⭐ Getting Back to the Basics

Many of the parents of children with autism whom I have worked with have expressed an urgency they feel in seeing their child develop within a certain time frame, trying to "beat the clock" before they lose the ideal "window of development." This can result in a feeling of in the background—or foreground—of your everyday life. Like a ticking clock: Tick. Tick. Tick.

This race against the clock is especially heightened at certain times of the year, such as birthdays, holidays or the beginning of a new school year. It is during these times that parents will often reflect on the past year and either be amazed by the growth in their child or disappointed that more was not achieved. This may also be a time when parents look at the year ahead with a heightened urgency to reach certain milestones as each year passes.

This relationship to time and your child, as you likely know, creates a huge amount of stress and pressure. Not only that, it often taints your relationship with your child, making it into something more like a time-sensitive project and making you feel more like a project manager than a parent.

I want to offer a paradigm shift in the way that you might relate to time and your child. What can help turn down the "tick tick tick" and create more calm and ease in your life and in the life of your child?

Get back to the basics. Here's what I mean:

Parents of children with autism often lose sight of their natural role as a parent and become project managers instead, tracking goals achieved and goals yet to achieve. What can get lost along the way is the relationship: the experience of enjoying your child, having nurturing moments where you are present with who your child is today, and honoring his unique interests or ways of doing things.

First and foremost, *you are a parent*—someone who is there to love your child for who he is and to respect his individual path in this world. When was the last time you:

- Simply enjoyed being with your child (whether reading a book, cuddling or running your fingers through the sand together)?

- Sat back and observed your child in wonder for who he is today, delighting in his unique interests, quirky sense of humor or incredible dexterity in a specific area?

- Spent time together with no goals in mind, other than to enjoy being together, even in total silence?

These are the basics of parenting that often get lost in the shuffle of IEP's and developmental check lists. These are the basics that get lost when your child's achievements override your relationship with your child.

Yes, developmental goals are important . . . But remember—especially as a new school year approaches and you might begin to hear the "tick tick tick" urgency of goals to be achieved in the upcoming year—that above all else, you are a parent of your child.

Take a moment to prioritize your relationship with your child *first* and the achievements you would like to witness in your child *next*.

Doing this takes you out of the construct of the race against the clock, since focusing on your relationship with your child happens *now,* in this very moment, no matter what skills your child is or is not demonstrating today.

Plus, interestingly, when your child senses that you are with him with ease, delight and no time pressure, you are cultivating the ultimate environment for true blossoming.

☆ Shifting Your Experience to the Now

The beginning of the Jewish new year is a time to connect to what is sacred in our lives. For me, it is a time to take a break from our endless "doing" and connect to "being." When I say being, I mean who we are right now, not who we want to become.

This seemingly simple task can actually be incredibly challenging. As a culture, we are continuously focused on moving forward, achieving something new, adding more accomplishments to our resume. We hope and believe that when we get "there," we will have arrived—at a place of infinite joy, peace and fulfillment.

In my work with families with autistic children, I have seen the same pattern magnified. I have heard many families tell me, "We will be happy when our child_____" (fill in the blank with the many things you might want for your child, like "when my child recovers," "when my child communicates," "when my child is toilet trained," etc.).

What happens is this: a child with autism is experienced as a work in progress, and many parents suffer from the endless desperation of getting "there," the place where their child's potential is truly actualized so they can finally be happy.

Does that sound familiar?

What I am about to say next might spark a lot of controversy, but I'm gonna say it anyway. *No matter what achievement your child makes, you will never arrive at happiness.*

What do I mean by that? I have seen parents who thought that happiness would come with their child's next achievement. They'd feel blessed or grateful to see their child recover or communicate or . . . until the next challenge came up. Will my child succeed academically? Will my child have a girlfriend? Why does my husband not listen when I talk? What is the purpose of my life now? How are we going to pay our bills?

The point is this: *You will never arrive at happiness because happiness is not a place to arrive; it is an experience to be cultivated.*

Joy can only be cultivated by embracing what *is*—who your child is today, right now, the very second that you are reading these words.

I am not suggesting that by accepting your child as he is, you should walk away from all bio-medical or therapeutic intervention. These therapies are incredibly powerful and have created momentous growth in children.

What I am saying is that as you do all that you do for your child, don't do it as if your life or happiness depend on it. In fact, I have seen that when you work toward helping your child without this type of desperation, you will actually be able to think more clearly and take more powerful and effective steps toward helping your child.

This is my wish for you in your new year: Don't wait until your child achieves X, Y or Z in order to experience peace and joy. This puts unnecessary stress on your child and keeps you from experiencing joy in this moment, the only place joy can truly be experienced. Instead, let your child experience you in a state of love and joy for who he is *right now* while you continue to be committed to his ongoing growth.

☆ Move Through Your Fear

Is fear something you struggle with: fear that your child will never speak, use a toilet or make a friend? If so, you are not alone.

But how do you move through your fear? Let me share a personal story with you:

This past year I have been working really hard with my 8-year-old son, Yonatan, to get to the root of his challenges with reading and writing. We have done occupational therapy, vision therapy, and horseback riding therapy. We have worked with a reading specialist, had an extensive assessment done, and are now doing Brain Highways® (which involves waking up with him at 5:30 am to do specific movements designed to help organize his brain).

He has grown to be more confident, social and independent. But has his reading improved? Well … Ummmm . . . Not really. At least, not yet.

As we moved past the halfway point of Brain Highways (and I still wasn't seeing an improvement in his reading), I started to feel myself getting more anxious and afraid: This was my last hope. We had tried *everything*. If this doesn't work, then what?

I set up a call with a staff member at Brain Highways, and she asked me a question that made a huge impact on me (the same question I often ask the families I work with but had forgotten to ask myself): "How would I feel if reading is never easy for Yonatan? How would I feel if this was something he would always struggled with?"

My answer: "I'd feel disappointed, frustrated and afraid."

Why? Because I believed that if he did not become more successful in reading, then he would always be held back and others would not see his true abilities (and he would not experience being seen in this way).

My bottom line fear was this: until he becomes more successful in reading, he will not be able to shine and bring his true potential to the world around him.

The conversation continued with me looking at that belief and challenging it. I sat with this belief and fear for several days and wrote and rewrote my interpretation.

Here is what I came to: Though I would love for him to excel in his reading and writing—and I will continue to work toward making that happen—I also realize that he is absolutely capable of finding ways to shine anyway. He is smart, kind, sensitive, creative and independent. And I do believe in his ability to develop his strengths and bring his special gifts to the world around him whether or not he can read with ease and fluency.

I began to see—and believe—that reading is not the total barrier to him actualizing his full potential that I once thought it was.

I cannot explain what a relief this was. It felt like a huge load had been lifted off my shoulders. Plus, this shift made a tremendous impact on him and us. Now, when he reads, I can listen with ease and patience, wanting more for him but not *needing* his fluency to come in order for him to fulfill his potential. Now, I can help him with love and determination but with no fear or stress.

Put simply, I can help him without being attached to the outcome.

Often, as we try to help our children, we are driven with fear, and that fear gets in the way of our child's growth and our relationship with him/her.

How can you turn that around? By looking at your biggest fear right in the face and diffusing it.

Here is a three-step system for letting go of fear:

1. Ask yourself, "How would I feel if my child never_____?"

Fill in the blank with whatever you fear most: never uses a toilet, never makes a friend, never speaks, etc. Ask the question you are most afraid to ask and do your best to sit with it and see what it feels like in your body. Identify how you feel.

2. Ask yourself, "Why do I feel this way?"

Here is where you are going to discover your beliefs about your child never developing that skill. For example, for me it was a fear that he would never be seen for his true abilities and that he would not experience being seen in that way. Take time with this one. Write your beliefs down until you get to the core belief that is driving your fear.

3. Challenge your belief.

You do this by asking these questions: Is that really true? What other options are there? What new belief can I replace the old one with so that I can come from a place of love and determination instead of fear and angst? For example, my new belief is: Yonatan does not need to read with fluency in order for him to bring his full self to the world around him. He can and will shine by developing his other strengths.

I don't mean to over simplify this process, but I do want to make it clear. Sit with each step, for days, even weeks, if you need to. Process it with someone or write it down. You may be surprised by much your how fear-based beliefs—which truly can be challenged and changed—are driving your path forward with your child.

Becoming aware of your fear, looking at it in the face and dropping it (and replacing it with a different belief instead) is a huge relief. I am not suggesting you give up on any of your goals. On the contrary, dropping your fears will instead allow you to push forward with clarity and to love and accept your child for who his is *today* while still believing in what he can become *tomorrow.*

You and your child will benefit greatly from this process. I know that Yonatan and I sure have.

☆ Forgive Yourself

Last night I went to a women's song circle in honor of the upcoming Jewish new year. As we began to sing, I realized that I felt a lump in my throat and heaviness in my chest. I was judging myself for something I had done earlier, and I just couldn't let it go.

Earlier that day I was planning on taking my kids to the mall to buy some new clothes for the holiday. They began to fight with each other and were being disrespectful, and so I told them we would not go to the mall if they could not treat me and each other with respect.

In response, my 7-year-old son came over to hug me and said, "I'm sorry." He looked up at me with these big puppy eyes.

And what did I do?

Deep breath; it's hard for me to even write this. I pushed him away and said, "I don't want apologies or hugs as a way to get what you want. That doesn't work for me. I am not interested in that kind of emotional manipulation."

I saw the rejected look in his face.

Ouch! What kind of person does that?

Yes, there was something in my message that I believed to be true, but how could I push my son away as he was apologizing and hugging me? How do I know whether he truly meant it or if it had been an attempt at emotional manipulation to go to the mall?

So I sat at the song circle and berated myself for being so unloving.

And that's when I came up with my intention for the year: to forgive myself. As I made that decision, my heart opened and I felt and instant release.

That is my intention for me and for you: to forgive ourselves, to see what we want to change and to manifest that change, but without judgment.

To forgive ourselves for:

- The moments—which we all share as parents—when we think, What kind of awful person am I?

- Having not done enough when he was younger (I hear this one all the time)

- Not doing more now (for example, "What about his diet?" or "Shouldn't I stay up until 2 a.m. to do more research online?")

- Not having patience (yes, I'm talking about yelling or saying things we wish had not come out of our mouths)

- Losing control (I'm talking about those moments no one wants to talk about, when we might have squeezed his arm too tight, hit, pulled or pushed)

- Thoughts we might have had (I worked with a mother who confessed that in her darkest times she had fantasies that her special child would have been a miscarriage or died in a car accident on the way home from school)

We are a community of parents. We have all done, said or thought things that we wish we hadn't, and we can carry that guilt with us for days, weeks, years or even the rest of our lives. That is an unfair burden when the challenges and demands of our lives can sometimes seem beyond our capacity. We are only human after all.

So now, in this moment, forgive yourself. Recognize that whatever you regret is a drop in the bucket compared to your endless dedication to your child.

And the amazing thing is that our children are always so much more forgiving of us than we are of ourselves. Often I will apologize to my children for something I feel terrible about, and they don't even remember what I did!

When you forgive yourself, you release a very heavy burden. When you release that heavy burden, you let love in and emanate love out. This love and open heart is what will give you the stamina you need on your journey with your child, and it is what will draw your child toward you.

So again, right now, forgive yourself.

☆ How to Navigate Through Daily Life

I sit here today, as I do every Thursday, to write and connect to my autism community. Every week I sit down, take a breath, quiet my mind and see what comes up. What is it I want to share? What is stirring in my heart today?

Sometimes I feel inspired, determined, moved and even goofy (yes, I have a totally goofy side, the side of me that has trained all three of my kids on the true art of pulling a good prank).

My intention is always to draw from whatever I feel that day and use that to offer thoughts, inspiration and guidance.

And today . . . Well, today I feel tender.

In case you don't know, I live in Israel. Without getting into the politics, I can say that the last couple of weeks here have been incredibly intense. Israeli and Palestinian children have been kidnapped and killed, riots on all sides have been spreading, and in the last couple of days, the situation has intensified with rockets, sirens and an all-out offensive.

Many tears have been shed on behalf of the families who have lost their children. I have experienced sorrow mixed with an intense desire for peace. I have felt fear as sirens go off and I gather my children into our protective shelter.

How have I navigated through this?

As one friend describes it, we keep flashing between "big picture" and "small picture."

Big picture: What will finally bring peace to the region?

Small picture: Camp is closed for my boys. Do I have the ingredients for the science experiment I wanted to do with them?

Big picture: How do I respond to the hate and discrimination I am reading in the media?

Small picture: Gotta change my son's occupational therapy appointment, and geez, that boy needs a haircut.

This is similar to what I know many of the parents with autistic children do to navigate through their life of multi-faceted challenges.

Big picture: How will he ever have a job?

Small picture: Wow, I cannot believe he licked a cucumber. He wouldn't even go near a vegetable just a year ago.

Big picture: Who will take care of him when I get older?

Small picture: Look how peaceful he is just running his fingers through the sand. What a special soul!

The point is, the big picture is important (I'm not saying it isn't), but the small picture, that's all we have in this moment.

That is what's happening, and the more I can connect to the joy of reading to my boys in our backyard campfire—even with the jets zooming overhead—the more I can breathe deeply and find peace within the madness. This is how I am able to access the tender and beautiful gifts even in a time of heaviness and hostility.

☆ How to Let Go of Anger

A mother I spoke to recently expressed that she really needed help to let go of her anger. Questions like "Why us?" or "Why did this happen to him?" keep her up at night and continue to feed the fire of anger—anger at god, anger at life, anger in general. Anger is one of the other most common emotional experiences parents have (and yes, overwhelm is on the top of that list as well).

Let me first address why it is important to deal with and let go of anger. Why not just carry that anger around while you do every therapy and diet under the sun for your child?

Reason #1. For your child. Anger burns fuel, and you simply don't have fuel to waste. If you continue to let anger rule your life, you will burn out and not have the stamina you need to go the distance with your child. Plus, if you are anger filled, you are blinded and unable to engage fully and deeply with your child (or all your children, for that matter), yet this is what your family needs most.

Reason #2. For you. You deserve a better life experience. Carrying anger around will affect your ability to sleep, your health, your digestive system and your relationships (anger can be ever so isolating). You have many years ahead of you; how do you want to live them?

So that's the *why,* and now the *how.* Here are three steps to let go of your anger and become more peaceful and present in your life:

1. Identify the anger.

This might sound crazy, but you may not even realize the extent to which you carry anger around all day—anger that your life is the way it is when your neighbor/sister/friend has it so easy or anger that your child has to work so much harder than everybody else. The first step is to set the intention to identify the anger. How does it feel in your body: in your shoulders, back or jaw? Become aware of the anger as you experience it and name it in the moment. For example: "I am watching my kid sit on the sidelines *again* and I feel angry. My jaws are clenched and my stomach is tight."

Tip: You can either say this to yourself or share it with someone you trust. You can also keep a journal where you write down the exact moment each day that you felt anger and what it felt like.

2. Decide whether you are ready to let it go.

This is important, because you may not be ready. Fair enough. You may want to hold on to that anger for now, and that is an important thing to recognize. Don't fight yourself on this one; you have enough battles as it is. Simply accept that you feel anger, that it's okay you feel anger, and continue to check in along the way to see whether you want to continue to hold on to it or let it go. However, do begin to notice how feeling anger impacts your life and your journey with your child. If you do want to overcome and let go of your anger, read on . . .

3. Discover the hidden gifts.

If you decide you are ready to let go of anger, then you can do so by making an intention to discover the hidden gifts in your child, exactly as he is right now, even if you want something else for him.

Quick story here: The first family I ever worked with recovered their son after an intensive four years of a home-based program and diet therapy. The mother had given up her job as a high-level lawyer to devote herself to working with her son. When she finally did put her son into a typical school, she was left with an empty feeling. She realized that she had been a part of one of the most meaningful journeys of her life; she had never felt so alive, so full of love and purpose. Though she was clearly so thrilled at how capable her son had become, she knew she just couldn't go back to being a lawyer. This was when the true gift of her journey became clear.

Ask yourself, Though I may want something different for him, what is a gift I can find in my child having autism (for him, for me, for our family, even for our community)?

Some examples may be:

- He is more sensitive to others who struggle.
- He is experiencing the true value in working hard to achieve a dream
- He has opened my heart and mind to loving what is different or hard for me to understand
- He has helped me not take for granted many things that other people don't even notice
- My daughter is more compassionate and understanding because of who her brother is.

Tip: Take time to really explore this by either writing it out or talking with a friend. Pick what resonates with you and begin to fill your heart, slowly, with the gratitude of the gift of your child. As you fill your heart with this kind of awareness and gratitude, you will begin to see your life differently—and there will be no more space left for your anger.

Then, as you work tirelessly to help your child communicate, make friends and learn life skills, you will do it with an open heart, driven by love and purpose instead of anger. You will feel the difference. Your child will feel the difference. Your whole family will feel the difference.

Bonus tip: Burn that anger out. Anger can be very toxic, and it is easiest to work through it if you can actively release it. This can be done with physical activity: running, dancing, yoga or housework (pulling those weeds out with all you've got!). Be aware as you do these activities that you are releasing anger to make more room for love and gratitude.

☆ Fear of the Future

The number one fear I hear from parents of children with autism is the fear of the future. Will he be independent? Will he be able to take care of himself? Will he get married, hold down a job and communicate? Who will take care of him when I am gone?

This fear of what will be and the questions surrounding this fear are the primary hot spots for parents with children on the autism spectrum. These questions often create an ongoing undercurrent of stress and anxiety on a daily basis—sometimes very subtle or sometimes downright debilitating.

As you probably know, this constant state of fear has a huge impact on your life, affecting your sleep, health and ability to be present with your family. I have even worked with families who were in such a daze of fear that they consistently ran through stop signs when driving.

I want to address this fear head on so you can create more calm, clarity and peace in your life.

How you feel is not secondary to your long "to do" list for your child. Your experience is primary, for it builds the foundation of the entire family.

I am not saying this to put additional pressure on you—or to make you feel more stressed about feeling stressed!—but to help you make the decision to give your experience some time and attention. You and your family need it. In truth, it is one of the most urgent things you can do.

But how? Here are three powerful ways to let go of fear:

1. Give the present moment your full attention.

I know this may sound overly simplistic, but this is where your power truly lies. We simply don't know what the future holds. You have no idea what your child's abilities will be in 10, 20, or 30 years. Plus, the world is changing so quickly that you also don't know what the options and opportunities will be for people with autism of varying degrees. Instead of using your energy imagining something you have no idea about, use your energy to connect with, support and inspire growth in your child today.

Tip: When you notice yourself worrying about the future, you can create a verbal mantra that you say to yourself, like, "All I know is who my child is today, and all I can do is love and help him now." You can also create a visual focus, like looking at a photo of you and your child, or mindfully observing his eyes, nose, lips, ears, fingers, etc., as a way to disrupt your worrying pattern and focus on the present moment.

2. See the kindness in the world.

One common fear parents have is, "Who will take care of my child if/when such and such happens?" As one mother expressed to me, she has been amazed at the many people who have come into her life since her son was diagnosed who are filled with kindness and compassion. The more you can take note of the people in your life who are kind and supportive, the more you can recognize and pray for those people to continue to come into your life and be there for your son when you need them.

Tip: It is easiest to do this if you surround yourself with positive messages and people. There are so many negative stories on the news and online surrounding autism, yet I know there are many more stories of miracles, achievements and communities gathering to support families. I do my best to share and post all those positive stories on my own Facebook page. I encourage you to do the same; limit the more negative news in your life (or even "de-friend" someone who constantly posts that kind of negative messaging).

3. Look the beast in the eyes.

This is a challenging one but can be very powerful for some. So much energy is spent imagining what life could be like for your child, and so many negative images may fill your mind. I spoke to a mom who found a wonderful respite home of caring people for her 22-year-old daughter with autism after years spent worrying about her daughter living in a home. This home had a warm, supportive staff and activities that her daughter loves, such as gardening and cooking. As you can imagine, this brought a huge amount of relief to the family.

If you hear of a *good* place in your area (like a social or vocational center), it may be helpful to go for a visit or at least learn more about it. This can help take the charge out of your "nightmare" by looking the beast in the eyes and seeing that it isn't such a horrible beast after all.

Anything and everything is possible for your child, including a healthy recovery. I have seen it with my own eyes. Yet along the way, you will likely have fears whispering (or yelling!) in your ears about the future. Continue to "go for the gold" and believe in every possibility for your child while simultaneously letting go of some of those fears (or even just the intensity of those fears). That way you will fully sink into your life with your child, have more energy and vitality, and more fully delight in your family.

Conclusion

As mentioned earlier in this book, our intention in writing *Play to Grow!* was to provide you with a manual of games to help your child grow to his fullest capacity within the most fundamental areas of social development. It is for this reason that each game has a specified goal. Each game was also designed to make it as likely as possible that your child will want to play these games with you, and therefore achieve the goals you have set.

It is important, however, to remember what is most important, and yet can be so easily forgotten. The specific skill addressed in each game is essential, but is not as important as the fact that you and your child are playing a game together. The most powerful results can stem from your child simply having fun and exciting interactions with you. The interaction itself will create an experience, and it is this experience—the joy and delight in being together—that will bring your child back for more. So above all else, make your play fun. Use your play to create a deep and meaningful connection with your child, because ultimately, there is no skill more important than your child's desire and ability to connect with another person. Achieving this close connection will open many doors, and it is from this desire that all other skills will grow.

Index of Games

Activity Toss, 36
Album of Friends, 87
The Alien Game, 95
All Mixed Up, 66
Alphabet/Number Strips, 153
The Amazing Maze, 155
The Amazing World of Nature, 84
Ambulance Ride, 33
Animal Charades, 68
Animal Surgery, 151
Appreciation Board, 133
Appreciation Presents, 132
Back to Back, 123
A Bag of Goodies, 58
Ball Pass, 147
Balloon Decorations, 154
The Balloon Hop, 145
Balloon Zip, 33
Balloons and Blankets, 39
Balloons Galore!, 61
Basketball Cheers, 38
Basketball Writing, 71
Basketball Writing (with a peer), 110
Beanbag Toss, 38
Beanbag Toss, 147
The Big Spin, 86
Bingo!, 75
Bingo (with a peer), 116
Birthday Blower Blow Out, 29
Blanket Breeze, 31
Blow Ball, 35
Blow Maze, 88
Blow Paint, 34
Body Language Charades, 95
Bounce Master, 48
Bubble Clap, 144
Bubble Master, 47
Bubbles, 34
Bye-Bye, 48
Calendar of Friends, 131
The Chain Game, 154
Charades, 45
Charades (with a peer), 110
Chutes and Ladders, 137
Circus Show!, 147
Click-Flash-Share!, 99
Cliff Hanger, 83
The Conversation Pass, 98
Conversation Starter, 100
Cooking Class, 103
Copy Me, 38
Cube Twister, 66

Daily Journal, 124
The Cushion Squish, 32
A Day at the Beach, 139
Doctor, 50
Doctor (Advanced), 60
Doctor (with a peer), 116
Drawing with Your Feet, 73
Drop!, 28
Fall Down, 34
Feed the Hungry Monster, 61
The "Feel Good" Spinner, 70
Feeling Album, 123
Feeling Box, 44
Fill in the Blank, 94
Fill Your Flower!, 76
Find the Hidden Treasure, 152
Follow the Leader (with a peer), 111
Freeze!, 36
Freeze and Switch!, 137
Freeze and Switch! II, 138
Freeze Together (with a peer), 113
Friendly Bus Driver, 90
Friendship Necklace, 153
Fun with Animals, 30
Fun with Face Paints!, 30
Fun with Stickers, 36
Funny Dolls, 42
The Funny Face Search, 63
Funny Hair Shop, 56
Game Sticks , 67
Get Me to My Carrot!, 94
Going to the Cleaners, 62
Guess What?, 58
Heavy, Heavy, Heavy! (with a peer), 112
Help a Friend, 104
Help a Friend (with a peer), 117
Help Me Find My Twin!, 156
Help Mr. Potato Head Get Dressed, 56
Hidden Picture, 155
Hot Debate, 128
Hot Dog Roll, 32
Hot Dog Roll (with a peer), 111
Hot Potato, 47
How Do You Measure Up?, 89
How Might You Feel?, 97
Huggy Cube, 51
The Human Jukebox, 37
I Can Dress Up All by Myself!, 153
I Spy with My Eye, 43
I'm a Rock Star!, 69
Instant Animals, 31
The Juggling Clown, 42

Jump Rope Snake, 29
Kid Soup, 46
Land/Sea, 145
The Laughing Drum, 49
Let's Go Camping!, 139
Let's Go Fishing! , 68
Let's Make a Deal!, 77
Let's Make Music!, 42
Lies or Truth?, 98
Lights, Camera, Action!, 96
Lip Reading, 100
Listening Game, 44
Mad Libs, 135
Magic Rocks, 69
Make a Face!, 96
Make Your Own Menu, 86
Makeover, 59
Making a Book, 72
Making Scenery, 87
Massage, 28
Memory with Feelings, 97
Morning and Night, 82
Mummy, 46
Mummy (with a peer), 112
A Museum of My Own, 126
A Museum of My Own II, 127
My Own Board Game, 74
My Own Memory Game, 75
My Very Own Bakery, 134
My Very Own Jewelry Shop, 134
Name That Tone, 129
New Shoes, 150
Noise Tube, 32
Obstacle Course, 146
Obstacle Course (with a peer), 115
Oh No, the Queen's Jewels!, 151
Our Amazing Bodies, 85
Pack Your Bags, We're Going on a
    Trip!, 103
Pass the Picture, 73
Pass the Present, 67
Pass the Prezzie (with a peer), 115
Pass the Prop, 70
Phone a Friend, 70
Pictionary, 135
Picture Story (with a peer), 117
Pin the Nose on Elmo, 72
Pin the Nose on the Face (with a
    peer), 113
Pizza Shop, 91
A Play of Your Own, 68

A Play of Your Own (with a peer),
    110
Problem Solving Agency, 128
Put a Puzzle Together (with a peer),
    116
Puzzle Time, 59
The Queen's Crown, 152
Quiet . . . Loud!, 63
Racecar Driver, 31
Red Light, Green Light, 46
Red Light, Green Light (with a
    Twist!), 43
Relay Races (with a peer), 113
Restaurant, 60
Restaurant (with a peer), 116
Ride Game, 35
Ring Jukebox, 37
Roll the Cube, 48
Roll the Cube (with a peer), 110
Safety Cat, 83
Seamstress, 151
Secret Box, 47
Secret Code, 89
Shape Match, 49
Shoe Store, 92
Show Me What You Got!, 64
Show-N-Tell, 124
Show-N-Tell II, 125
Show-N-Tell (with a peer), 119
Silly Animal Mix-Up, 65
Silly Faces, 57
Silly Skits, 82
The Singing Game, 30
Slow . . . Fast!, 64
Smelling Game, 45
Smelly Socks!, 150
The Snake Chase, 144
The Sneeze Spot, 76
Spell Master, 93
Spin the Bottle, 51
Spin, 28
Stand Up Comedy, 130
Stand Up Comedy II, 131
Stories in My Life (with a peer), 118
A Story of 3 Words, 74
Stranded on a Desert Island, 138
Superhero Interview, 91
The Surprise Sneeze, 101
Talking Stick (with a peer), 118
Tea Party, 49
Tell Me What You See, 55

Thank You Cards, 132
Things I Like, 133
Three-Way Conversation Pass, 130
Tickle Roll, 37
Tickles, 33
Tie Me Up, Cowboy!, 50
Time's Up!, 99
Toy Store, 55
Trivia Game Show, 136
Tug of War, 144
We Are on a Mission! (with a peer),
    114
What Goes Together?, 102
What Is Behind Picture #1?, 62
What Is Different?, 57
What Is in the Box?, 63
What's Different about Me?, 101
What's Missing?, 45
What's Missing from This Picture?,
    57
What's Wrong Here?, 102
When, Where, Who?, 81
When, Where, Who? (Advanced), 81
Where Are We Now?, 129
Where Is the Circle?, 58
Whose Voice Is That?, 44
Word Search, 88
Yoga!, 73
Yoga! (with a peer), 112
The Yoga Play, 146
The Yoga Spin, 145
Your Own Board Game (with a peer),
    117
Your Own Fashion Show, 85
Your Very Own Comic Strip, 127
A Zoo of My Own, 125
A Zoo of My Own II, 126

About the Authors

Tali Berman is an autism specialist and developmental play expert and has worked with hundreds of children from over 30 different countries since 1997. She has authored *Play to Grow,* which was voted as one of the top five resources by the *Special Needs Book Review,* is now sold in four languages, and has proven to be an invaluable resource for families worldwide.

Tali is also the founder/leader of the annual "Autism Empowerment Telesummit," where she has gathered top autism experts on her elite panel (including Temple Grandin, Jenny McCarthy and Donna Gates), reaching thousands of families annually around the globe. She has contributed regularly to some of the most well-read autism publications, including the Generation Rescue blog and *The Autism File* magazine.

Tali currently lives with her husband and three children in Israel.

Visit www.taliberman.com to learn more about Tali's global training and coaching programs and to receive her weekly blog.

Abby Rappaport has worked as an enthusiastic play therapist for autistic children since 2002. Having grown up with a special needs brother, she has a unique perspective on both the strengths and challenges of someone with special needs. Abby resides in Israel.